The Winds of Change

an autobiography
of South Dakota State University's
last Dean of Women

By Vivian V. Volstorff

The Winds of Change

an autobiography
of South Dakota State University's
last Dean of Women

By Vivian V. Volstorff

Co-Editors:
Jana L. (Pedersen) Petersen
James O. Pedersen

South Dakota State University Alumni Association

W*inds of Change* is dedicated to all my former South Dakota State University students. May they continue to be goal and service oriented and discover the true happiness that comes with sharing what they have learned with others.

When I came to South Dakota State in June 1958, it was with the key question of what support staff would I find. My fears were soon allayed. There were some very outstanding incumbents and certainly among the most outstanding were the Dean of Women, Dean Vivian Volstorff, and the Dean of Men, Dean "Prof" Walder. Not only were they both outstanding in their own right, but they worked together as a strong team to provide the students with the finest kind of leadership. This was the sixth campus on which I had been located and I had never seen their equal. Dean Volstorff had taken her post as a young woman just out of graduate school, in 1932. Charles W. Pugsley, then President, had been involved in her selection and had provided the young lady with leadership and with the administrative support to develop. And develop she had—to become the outstanding Dean of Women that I have known.

Hilton M. Briggs

Dean Volstorff not only had the confidence and support of the students; it was fair to say, "most of the girls really loved her." Yes, and she had the admiration of the young men. She truly helped with the social life of the campus, was innovative, and a hard worker. She was always thinking of how campus life could be improved.

Furthermore, the Dean of Women was highly respected and appreciated by members of the faculty, citizens of the community, and by the graduates she had nurtured when they were in school. No matter where you went, you were asked about her and there was always a note of appreciation of what she had meant in their lives. She was a great teacher of history, but they weren't referring to academics. Her enrichment of their lives went far beyond a role in the classroom.

You will be thrilled to read *THE WINDS OF CHANGE*. It is a portrait of the influence of a great lady on the lives she touched in 41 years of distinguished service. She has been honored in so many ways and the ballroom of the Union bears her name. But neither honor, nor a book can describe all she did at South Dakota State University as she so effectively touched the lives of thousands.

Hilton M. Briggs
President Emeritus
South Dakota State University
President: 1958-1975

What a sight! What is it? Believe it or not—right in the middle of a Land Grant college campus! A group of co-eds engaged in an annual Spring Rite, dancing, prancing and cavorting around a decorated pole. "Gee," said one of the visiting prospective freshman strolling up the Medary Avenue sidewalk, "this is an Ag college. You'd think they'd be putting up a pole barn instead of a May Pole."

Yes, things had been astir on the campus since the arrival of the new, young Dean of Women, Vivian Virginia Volstorff. Fresh out of one of the more elite universities in the Big Ten, Northwestern University, she had laid out a challenging agenda for South Dakota State College and herself. In addition to building on her profound interest in history, Dr. Volstorff was intent on raising the cultural ambience and intellectual outlook on the State College campus.

Sherwood O. Berg

The new Dean of Women concentrated on developing and bolstering the areas of leadership, scholarship, and service. The ideals that she embraced and the strategies that she mapped out fit nicely into the overall Land Grant philosophy. Moreover, her moves were timely. The Land Grant colleges, such as State College, needed an inspirational force. SDSC had pulled itself out of the economic depression and the Dust Bowl of the thirties; it had "marched off" to the Great War with the rest of the country in the forties; it had to handle the burgeoning enrollments of the returning GIs and the increased female students in the fifties and later decades.

Dean Volstorff's concern for student-organized and student-managed organizations led to many positions of meaningful leadership on campus. Her attention, and that of her colleague, Professor Orlin E. Walder, Dean of Men, meant that student governance, through the Board of Control, and student social and cultural life, under the Student Union Board of Managers, were student operated. The programs were products of student expression, inputs, and implementation, not programs sponsored by the administration or the faculty. Scholarship received a great deal of attention. Not only was individual scholarship enhanced, but student and faculty organizations, such as Mortar Board and the American Association of University Women, were encouraged to recognize scholarship as an important and integral part of academic life. Permeating all of Dr. Volstorff's efforts was the concept of voluntary service on the part of students in the development of resident and academic life. You will note this refrain repeated time and again as you read of Dr. Volstorff's experiences. She believed in "service above self." She would have made a wonderful Rotarian!

Dr. Volstorff was an excellent and highly disciplined instructor. She taught courses in *Contemporary Europe* and *The Contemporary World*. After WWII, veterans flocked to her classes, wanting to know the likely emerging world geopolitics following the experiences that they had been through. Dr. Volstorff had kept a huge file on WWII events. She was aware of some of the differences in reporting among the war correspondents. On occasion, to clarify issues in these differing dispatches, she would open discussions regarding important battles in the various WWII zones. She would cite interpretations of the basic strategy employed by each side, the maneuvers attempted, relative strength of forces, the use of reserves, the effect on the local population, troop morale, and the like. Invariably, she elicited a reaction from the veterans in the class. Once in awhile she would challenge the views of a veteran. Jim Dunn, Bryan Baughman, or Bob Barnes would likely protest and say, "But, Dr. Volstorff, I was there!" She would quietly close her folder and proceed. She had gotten what she wanted.

Virtually every student on campus during Dr. Volstorff's tenure has some memory of her myriad of efforts at social enlightenment. In retrospect, they were enjoyable: teas, formal dinners, receptions, introductions, "cozies," and of course, the May Pole dance. And the famous Volstorff hats! I recall an item in a mid '40s SDSC yearbook. The *Jack Rabbit*, reporting on the annual banquet of the Student Board of Control held in the Pugsley Union, noted that Miss Volstorff wore one of her hat creations and that she was jabbed in the coiffure twice by a fellow who mistook her bonnet for his vegetable salad.

True, the winds of change are capricious. But Dr. Volstorff rose above them. She was a beacon. A beacon high over the prairie that beamed a clear message that those young men and women, who had the privilege of attending an institution of higher learning, had assumed special professional, community and personal responsibilities. She was a hardheaded observer of the winds of change. On the crucial issues of preparing young persons for productive lives and of how the college or university should go about aiding and abetting that process, she did not remain a slave of her hopes, her dreams, or her passions. She was a "doer," a mover and a shaker. She got things done—and we as students loved doing them with her.

Sherwood O. Berg
President Emeritus
South Dakota State University

Student: 1940-43; 1946-47
President: 1975-1984

ACKNOWLEDGEMENTS

Many persons have contributed to the creation and development of *THE WINDS OF CHANGE...AN AUTOBIOGRAPHY OF SOUTH DAKOTA STATE UNIVERSITY'S LAST DEAN OF WOMEN.*

Obviously, and most importantly, Vivian V. Volstorff is to be applauded for the manuscript she created for this book. She diligently recorded and composed this student-centered, 1932-1973 history of South Dakota State University. On April 28, 1973 Dean Volstorff concluded her retirement dinner remarks with..."I've loved my life at State—all 41 years and the many, many students who made my life's work worthwhile." This book tells the stories that defined her unforgettable career as Dean of Women. It is a history that captures the unique and undeniable spirit of South Dakota State University students. That spirit, which Dean Volstorff helped to build, continues today in the happenings, the achievements, the loyalties and the generosities of South Dakota State University's alumni.

That spirit is clearly evident in students' memories of Dean Volstorff. Thanks to seven former SDSU students representing the span of years Miss Volstorff served as Dean of Women who shared their memories in the Epilogue: Eleanor Christopherson Cranston Roscoe, Robert Karolevitz, Susan Smith Schutz, Patricia Clancy Leiferman, Barbara Strandell and Susan Stockwell Olson. Dean Volstorff recognized these former students as examples of the greatest reward from her career... students who cared and shared with other students the life succeeding lessons they learned while at SDSU.

Other individuals who helped make this publication come to life include: Co-editor Jana (Pedersen) Petersen, my daughter, who, despite a new baby and a challenging career, accepted and delivered on the challenge of transforming Dean Volstorff's memories into very readable book form. Former SDSU Presidents Hilton M. Briggs and Sherwood O. Berg for the cogent administrative perspectives offered in the Preface. Tricia Jill Velure for her scholarly Introduction. Dean Volstorff was one of four former female college administrators that Ms. Velure interviewed, analyzed and presented for her Masters Thesis in History at NDSU. Dawn

Stephens, SDSU's Agricultural Heritage Museum Archivist, whose competent and persevering efforts converted dozens of Jack Rabbit imprints and University photos into quality images that compliment many of the stories of individuals highlighted in this book. The unidentified Jack Rabbit photographers who recorded the dozens of images which compliment the manuscript. Pam Merchant for her creative cover design. VJ Smith, Executive Director of the SDSU Alumni Association, and David Marquardt, Executive Director of the SDSU Foundation, who in conjunction with their sponsoring organizations gave abiding support and related funding guarantees that made the publishing process happen. Vice President Michael Reger who arranged for his Secretary, Beth Clapp, to make the conversion of Dean Volstorff's hand written notes to electronic Word files. Vice President Carol Peterson for her encouraging support and the work of her Administrative Assistant Mary Reeter, who helped with manuscript copying and work-study logistics. Holly Hanson who brought her computer focused work-study student skills to assist with pre-publication details. Thanks also to Patrick Leary for final proof reading and to DJ Cline, Elizabeth Williams, and the Alumni Office staff for their help in planning for and supporting the marketing of *The Winds of Change*.

James O. Pedersen, Co-Editor

CONTENTS

DEAN VOLSTORFF WITH CO-EDITORS

Dean Volstorff with Co-Editors, Jana (Pedersen) Petersen and James O. Pedersen at Brookview Manor in Brookings, SD on July 18, 2000. (Elizabeth Williams photo)

INTRODUCTION

VIVIAN V. VOLSTORFF
By Tricia Jill Velure
From Masters Thesis—
A PLACE FOR WOMEN ON MEN'S COLLEGE CAMPUSES:
PROFESSIONAL WOMEN AT NORTHERN PLAINS LAND-GRANT COLLEGES

Tricia Jill Velure

The author interviewed Vivian Volstorff twice in 1998 to prepare this as part of her master's thesis at North Dakota State University. Four micro-cassette recordings of the interviews are available for review at the H. M. Briggs Archives/Special Collections at South Dakota State University.

In the summer of 1932, when Dr. George Lincoln Brown, Dean of the College and the Division of General Science at South Dakota State College, welcomed Vivian Volstorff to Brookings, he brought to State a "most unusual woman," a 25-year-old Dean of Women.

While the young Volstorff was not the motherly or worldly type that many people were expecting from State's new dean of women, she proved over the next 41 years that she was worthy of the title. She knew that her students' adult lives would be the measuring stick of her accomplishments. Only by turning out well-educated, goal- and service-oriented women students did she believe she could claim success. She thus worked unceasingly to prepare State's young women for productive, fulfilling futures. She wanted the male-dominated, land-grant college that existed in 1932 to become an environment that no longer would overlook women's education. Today, the 93-year-old is confident that she performed her job well. Because gender and the limitations of the land-grant system did not discourage her, she fulfilled a vision of what a campus should be and what a women's program should be. This vision, she believed, was her responsibility to her students and the world.

Vivian Virginia Volstorff was born in Chicago in 1907. Her father was a businessman, but he also was a gifted artist and violinist and spoke several languages. Her mother had attended business college but married before earning a degree. Volstorff's sister and only sibling, Olive, was born in 1912. Volstorff learned to love reading and learning at an early age, encouraged by her father who brought her books from the library and by an aunt who was a high school teacher. Throughout her schooling, Volstorff's teachers were amazed at the amount of history she knew.

Volstorff graduated from Elgin High School in Chicago in 1924. Later that year, she entered Elgin Academy, the local junior college. She was encouraged in her academic pursuits by Hugh Renny, a history professor and drama coach, who likely helped her to get a scholarship to the prestigious Northwestern University in 1925. That scholarship became the first of several she received while at Northwestern. She also was awarded two history fellowships and served as a tutor in several women's dormitories there. Volstorff graduated with a Bachelor of Science degree in History in 1928 and a Master of Arts degree in History and Political Science in 1929. She then entered the doctoral program at Northwestern. Her dissertation, directed by her adviser, Dr. I.J. Cox, was on William C. C. Claiborne, the first governor of Louisiana. In the summer of 1930, she attended summer school at Harvard and conducted research at the Library of Congress in Washington, D.C. She also became thoroughly grounded in the cultural and political affairs of the East and Washington. Guided by Major Green, a retired Army officer, who was a friend of Dr. Cox, she attended embassy affairs, art exhibits and museums. In 1932, she completed her doctorate degree and sought work as a history professor.

At the time, the number of history professors exceeded the number of positions available, Dean McGraw, the Dean of Women at Northwestern encouraged Volstorff to consider other careers, including the opportunity at State. The dean merely thought that the more options Volstorff pursued, the more likely she was to find a job in those depressed economic times. Volstorff also could have accepted a position at Northwestern or one of several women's colleges, but she saw the male-dominated campus in Brookings as a bigger challenge for advancing women's education. Although she did not abandon her dream of becoming a history professor, Volstorff took the dean's advice and moved to Brookings, accepting the Dean of Women position, with a salary of $2,200.

She took up residence at Wecota Hall, one of the three women's dormitories on the campus. Although she did not pay for her apartment, she did pay for meals in the cafeteria, which cost $3 to $4 a week, according to the South Dakota State College of Agriculture and Mechanic Arts *Bulletin* of April 1933. Volstorff's office was adjacent to her apartment.

Coming from a more liberal environment in the East, Volstorff experienced culture shock in her new home. Here she was, trying to educate and improve young women at a land-grant college in a state where many farmers, a large percentage of the population, could think of no reason for women to even attend college. Rather than accepting that attitude, Volstorff made it a point to help State grow beyond its "cow college" moniker.

However bewildered she was by the lack of interest in women's education, some of her colleagues made her feel welcome at the college, including President Pugsley. He feared that because the Dean of Women was new and young, her ideas might be overlooked by the faculty. He told her that until she felt established on the campus, she could share her ideas with him, and if he believed they had merit, which he often did, he would recommend them to the faculty. In her early days at State, many of Volstorff's ideas were implemented that way.

Although she served the college in many capacities, her primary role was as Dean of Women. All female students whose homes were not in Brookings were required to live on campus unless they received formal permission from the housing committee to live elsewhere. Volstorff was in charge of these women, regardless of where they resided. In 1934-1935, the first academic year of Volstorff's tenure for which statistics are available regarding enrollment and gender, she was dean of 245 women.

The three women's dormitories existed when Volstorff arrived on campus grew to five by the time she retired in 1973. Volstorff herself lived on campus until the Army and Air Force required all dormitory space available in 1942-1943. The *Bulletin* reported in December 1943, "The civilian students, both men and women, were all housed in private homes, except the freshmen women, who lived in rooming houses under supervision of the Dean of Women and her assistants." After World War II, Volstorff continued to live off campus and was assisted by head residents in the dormitories. Her duties, however, were not lessened by this move, nor did she want them to be.

As Dean of Women, Volstorff found herself working in five main areas: supervising female students, which diminished as college women gained more freedom in the 1960s and 1970s; counseling; arranging housing; assisting in job placement; and most importantly, directing the social programs. Volstorff placed less emphasis on rule enforcement and more on encouraging participation, reflecting a national trend toward gradually slackening rules for women on college campuses. Volstorff, who combined traditional manners with forward thinking, wanted her students to become ladies, but she saw no limits in regard to what they could become professionally. She wanted women to participate in careers of their own choosing, in professional organizations and in women's organizations. The best way to prepare women for those things, Volstorff thought, was to give them opportunities to participate in activities and organizations while in college.

With her primary duty as Dean being to plan activities, Volstorff set about coordinating open houses, teas, dinner parties and dances. This at first may seem like a frivolous and simple responsibility, but Volstorff took it seriously. Activities were intended to be more than just fun, but also an opportunity to instill in students the importance of poise, etiquette, graciousness, dedication, service and education outside the classroom. The high standards Volstorff set for her students were instilled not only through activities but also through the organizations that sponsored the activities.

In her post as social program coordinator, Volstorff made some of her biggest and most enduring contributions to State and women's education. Volstorff's achievements may seem instead like her students' accomplishments, but she and the students shared these dreams and made them come true together. The establishment of State chapters of Alpha Lambda Delta, Mortar Board and the American Association of University Women were the result of Volstorff's hard work—and lost vacation time. Volstorff believed the sole reason she was at State was to improve the lives of students both during and after their college days. She was to give students a vision in life and to help them to move toward their goals. Volstorff's personal goal was an unselfish one: to make the world a better place by instilling high standards, liberal ideals and leadership qualities in a small segment of the world's population. While it was mainly the students who reaped the benefits of Volstorff's work, she took satisfaction in knowing that she was instrumental in furthering women's lives and education.

Her first major accomplishment was the establishment of Women's Day at State, beginning in 1933, with sponsorship from Sigma Lambda Sigma, the senior women's honor society. On this day of festivities, female students were recognized for their scholarship, leadership and service to the college. If the young women received more acknowledgment, Volstorff believed, they would be encouraged to work harder and set higher standards. Over the years, Women's Day became a renowned event. In the 1954 college yearbook, *The Jack Rabbit*, the coverage of Women's Day was titled, "Co-eds Conquer Campus." The 1955 *Jack Rabbit* stated that on Women's Day, the female students "had their chance to prove that although a minority on the campus, they certainly were not to be overlooked." Patronizing as the writings were, they alluded to the importance of the occasion to women at State. It was the biggest day of the year for many of them and later was expanded to involve more women, including outstanding women scholars from the various colleges on campus, prominent female student leaders and beauty queens. In the 1960s, Women's Day began to feature nationally known female speakers.

Volstorff's second major accomplishment as the social program coordinator was attaining a student union. Soon after her arrival at State, she began arguing that it was awfully difficult to have a social program without a proper place to host social events. What the college needed, she told President Pugsley, was a student union. Pugsley agreed but knew it was financially unfeasible. But in the late 1930s, Pugsley secured funding through a Public Works Administration grant and long-term bonding. With the work of a planning committee on which Volstorff served, her dream came true. The union, completed in 1940, included rooms suitable for a variety of social occasions that Volstorff deemed important, and she soon became responsible for furnishing it as well. She also helped to plan the Christy Ballroom addition to the union in 1957 and a second student union, which was completed in 1973 and contains a ballroom named after her.

Her third significant achievement in social programs was attaining a chapter of Alpha Lambda Delta, the national organization for freshmen women scholars. Local recognition of the freshmen women on Women's Day was considerate but short-lived. National recognition of their achievements seemed a more enduring symbol of their scholarship and an opportunity for them to begin participating in an organizational setting. Like Women's Day, Alpha Lambda Delta also was viewed as a motivational tool, as membership required a grade point average of at least a 3.5 on a 4.0 scale. Volstorff and Sigma thus worked diligently to attain this highest means of distinction for freshmen women's scholarship. Alpha Lambda Delta was installed at State in the spring of 1967.

Volstorff's fourth major accomplishment as the social program coordinator came when Sigma was accepted as a chapter of Mortar Board. When Volstorff arrived at State in 1932, Sigma had existed at the college for only a year and needed a purpose, she believed. As with the other activities in which Volstorff was involved, she gave Sigma a purpose almost immediately by assigning the students to assist her guidance work with incoming freshmen. Because of the great emphasis she always placed on the "service motif," Volstorff was especially proud of the Sigma counselors for the many hours they volunteered. But the volunteer work was just a small step toward Sigma's acceptance as a chapter of Mortar Board. Believing that persistence would bring them the ultimate recognition and pride, Volstorff challenged Sigma members to reach ever higher levels of scholarship, leadership and service. She helped Sigma to move closer to Mortar Board status by promoting freshmen women's scholarship; namely, sponsoring Women's Day, funding a freshmen women's scholarship, and helping to establish a chapter of Alpha Lambda Delta. Providing tutor services and sponsoring symposiums on such subjects as human sexuality, women's liberation and Native American awareness also were important. Finally, after 40 years of hard work, the ones Volstorff proudly called "my Sigma girls" qualified as a local Mortar Board chapter in 1972. Perseverance had paid off, just as Volstorff had predicted.

As important as those several accomplishments were to Volstorff's career and her students, what she considers her biggest achievement stemmed from her work beyond the position as Dean of Women. It was gaining accreditation of State from the American Association of University Women, or AAUW. Founded in 1881, AAUW sought to broaden women's opportunities in higher education and professional employment. The Brookings chapter of AAUW was established in 1931, but State graduates could become only associate members because they did not meet the national organization's only membership requirement: being a female graduate from an accredited college. State held only provisional recognition from AAUW, contingent upon becoming accredited by the American Association of Universities. As an active AAUW member and a conscientious Dean of Women, Volstorff sought to do whatever was necessary to make State an institutional member of AAUW. Although it surely was not a specific duty of hers, acquiring the membership defined what being the Dean of Women was all about in Volstorff's mind—instilling in female students the importance of lifelong education and participation.

Women's Day and the Student Union represented progress toward AAUW membership but were not enough. In regard to female employees and students, it could come only by improving State's programs for women through better athletics, more liberal arts majors, better health services, more women in administrative positions and higher salaries. Volstorff could not find the money necessary to accomplish such initiatives, so in

1940, the American Association of Universities denied State accreditation. Thus, State lost its provisional recognition from AAUW and with it went the opportunity for State graduates to join the organization.

Volstorff, however, was not defeated. She continued to struggle to meet the requirements for accreditation, particularly while serving as the president of the Brookings AAUW chapter from 1947 to 1949. In 1948, the American Association of Universities discontinued accrediting colleges, and the AAUW Committee on Standards and Recognition began to decide whether to accept colleges applying for AAUW approval. Acting on behalf of State and the Brookings AAUW, Volstorff appealed for the accreditation of State at the national AAUW convention in 1949. Dr. Ruth Boynton, a standards committee member, officially inspected the college in the spring of 1950, and AAUW gave full recognition to State that same year.

The significance of AAUW approval was that it recognized the college for having made a commitment to providing a high quality working environment for woman employees and a commendable educational environment for female students. As a stronger female presence was felt on campus, the "cow college" image that Volstorff had long battled began to fade. State was becoming less of a traditional, male-centered college and more of a liberal-minded, multi-faceted university—officially named South Dakota State University in 1964. Setting such a good example for the female students was important to Volstorff. After all, if they came from an institution of high ideals and open minds, she believed they would carry the standards with them and strive throughout their lives for greater equality for women.

As her work for AAUW indicated, Volstorff gave her full effort to everything she did. That included her teaching, in which she was extremely disciplined and confident. "I was very sure about my history business, because I had taught at Northwestern for two years," she affirmed. "You know I'd made the grade." At State, she proved herself again. During World War II, when the male history professors were busy with the Army and Air Force on campus, Volstorff taught the greatest variety of courses of her tenure: Contemporary Europe, English History, Bibliography and Criticism, and the American West. Throughout most of her career, Volstorff taught either Contemporary Europe or Contemporary World, both upper level History courses, and Reading in Current Affairs, a lower level History course.

Her teaching methods were unconventional for the time in which she taught, as her students, she said, "had to read a lot. ... They had to react to it. There were certain questions they had to answer about it. They had to think to answer these questions. And that was unheard of. Nobody had ever made them do that kind of thing before. And that contributed to the fact that they thought I was a pretty strict teacher."

Volstorff required students in Reading in Current Affairs to subscribe to the *New York Times* and used it as a teaching tool, which she thought would give students a thorough grounding in world thought, politics and culture. Being well-informed on current domestic and foreign issues was Volstorff's aim for herself and her students, because she realized how small the world was becoming. Understanding fascism, communism and world religions would be useful for the future. While taking her course, students might have considered her too demanding, but she firmly believed that many of them would appreciate later the discipline she had over herself and her classes. In fact, she knew several students who continued their subscriptions to the *New York Times* even after they had finished her class.

Volstorff also reached a great number of students through her freshmen orientation lectures, in which she introduced the freshmen to the qualities that would help to bring them success not only as professionals but also as citizens of communities and the world. She discussed personal and professional relationships, college and workplace expectations, and the importance of participating in events and organizations. She also demonstrated table etiquette and ballroom dancing. It pleased Volstorff to present the lectures, because she was concerned that State too often emphasized technical training at the expense of instruction on humanity, society and culture. By complementing technical knowledge with social enlightenment, Volstorff was convinced that she was helping to develop good, liberal minds and future leaders.

As the Dean of Women, as a professor and also as a public speaker, Volstorff tried to stimulate intellectual life and world awareness. She thought of that task as one of the biggest challenges facing her at State and in South Dakota in general. Encouraging local residents to broaden their viewpoints on foreign affairs was difficult. But as Volstorff said, "I felt it was my duty to combat that isolationism." She believed that absolute preparedness was the key to making her speeches count, so she stayed current on world events and scholarly thought. She made 25 to 30 speeches every year, usually on international relations, to a variety of audiences. They included such titles as, "The Political Situation in France," given in the 1936-1937 academic year; "Russian Problems," given in 1943 or 1944; and "The American Profile," presented in 1956.

Volstorff spoke "to straighten out the international situation, but also to influence the feeling that some people had about a cow college," she said. That image of State hurt Volstorff personally, as she had worked so diligently to assure women the best education possible and all of her students a background in liberal ideas and world events. It is not surprising, then, that she gave many speeches on the importance of and trends in women's education.

In addition to all of these responsibilities and activities, Volstorff advised the Young Women's Christian Association, the Women's Self-Government Association, the Women's Dorm Council, University Dames, and the International Relations Club. She was an active member of the Board of Control, which regulated State student activities; the campus branch of Pi Gamma Mu, which was an honor society for social scientists; and the Brookings Women's Club. She also held memberships to the American Historical Association, the National Association of Deans of Women and Counselors, and the South Dakota Association of Deans and Counselors. In the state division of AAUW, she was chairwoman of international relations for four years, second and first vice-president for four years, and president for two years.

Vivian Volstorff was fortunate, at a time when most women her age never attended college, to experience nothing but support to become a scholar from her family, school teachers and college professors. She was among only 383 American women to earn a PhD in 1932. The activities and achievements on her way to a PhD were impressive. Considering Volstorff's experiences before she began her career in Brookings, perhaps it should come as no surprise that she became an accomplished Dean of Women, professor and public speaker. But, as Volstorff realized soon after arriving at State, the lack of interest in liberal ideas and women's education was even more glaring than she had anticipated. As John E. Miller, a colleague of Volstorff's on the State history faculty, wrote: "The idea of having a newly minted PhD, hardly older than many of her charges, put into such a demanding position, would have struck trepidation into less determined creatures. But no one ever accused Vivian Volstorff of being timid. Making her presence felt immediately, she brought to campus a cosmopolitan intelligence and unassuming personality that made her an unforgettable presence for two generations of students." Miller's comments were published in *Centennial of SDSU 1881-1981*, published by State in 1982.

Improving women's education would prove to be no small task at a land-grant college. Even with the support of men like President Pugsley, achieving higher status for college women would require determination. Nothing was handed to Volstorff—she earned her accomplishments.

A major reason for her success was her attitude. Because she personally did not feel that she had ever been discriminated against as a female, other than in salary, she did not use womanhood as an excuse for complacency. In addition, instead of viewing challenges as limitations that she could not overcome, she approached them as opportunities waiting to be explored.

The basic challenges that Volstorff faced were the shortcomings of the land-grant college system itself. She particularly was concerned that technical programs were emphasized at the expense of the liberal arts and world affairs and that women's education often was given secondary consideration. As evidenced by accomplishments such as Women's Day and the AAUW accreditation, which included women of all majors and professions, as well as by teaching and public speaking, Volstorff challenged some of the shortcomings she found at State. She introduced culture and current world affairs into the lives of South Dakotans and gave women students the tools to live productive lives as citizens and professionals. Those tasks were not easy. Volstorff nonetheless was glad to tackle them, because they offered her the chance to make a difference in people's lives.

But not Volstorff's entire career was about triumph. Like many women, she witnessed lower salaries for women doing work comparable to that of men. This problem, which certainly is not confined to the land-grant college system, reflects general discrimination against women and remains even after Volstorff retired. She also was disheartened by societal changes present at State and elsewhere during the 1960s and 1970s. Volstorff is an understanding woman, but she was not prepared to address or counsel students about the movement of alcohol and drugs onto the campus. She also noticed a loss of interest in service organizations, formal gatherings and culture that she had worked so hard to build.

There were still limitations for professional women in the land-grant college system up to the time Volstorff retired in 1973. But Volstorff witnessed much change for women during her tenure. Ladylike behavior and the women's sphere were no longer focuses in her job. She promoted etiquette but did not preach it; she supported women's wanting to be homemakers and teachers but also encouraged engineers and chemists with equal enthusiasm. She had enough career opportunities to be considered one of the first truly modern women educators.

For 41 years, Volstorff lived women's education at State. Granted, if she had not come along or stayed, another Dean of Women likely would have fulfilled this role. But would she have been an equal role model? Volstorff's manners were impeccable, her education unrivaled, and her desire to understand and help students ceaseless. She also enjoyed seeing improvements in the status of women in society. How fitting it was, then, that Volstorff was State's last Dean of Women. By 1973, the University saw that women no longer needed to be confined to a single role on campus, complete with a dean, as they did when Volstorff began her career. College men and women were more equal than ever before, and thus could share a dean, an activities director and all other positions once separated by the deans of men and women posts. The *"Winds of Change"* that Volstorff has authored reflects a period of women's education that ended at a time when the subject no longer was viewed as an issue apart.

FROM CHICAGO TO BROOKINGS IN 1932

Dean Volstorff as shown in the 1934 Jack Rabbit. The new Dean of Women and the first PhD prepared History Professor. (1934 Jack Rabbit photo)

WELCOME TO STATE

"We are certainly glad to see that you're still alive," said one of two gentlemen darting toward me at a South Dakota State University alumni recognition dinner in the autumn of 1980. At 73 years young, I was rather startled by this remark.

"We saw the plaque at the entrance to the ballroom of the new union," one of the men explained, "and we thought that you had died in 1973."

That was my retirement date, I told them, after 41 wonderful years at State.

The two were from Chicago and had returned to the reunion as members of the 1935 football team, which beat the University of Wisconsin Badgers 13-6.

We reminisced about the silk football pants the players received from Charles E. Coughlin in recognition of the team's victory over Wisconsin, and I reminded them of the calf they had "borrowed" and butchered. They had dined well for several weeks during the dismal depression days, only to learn their dinners were not of calf but rather pig, one of Professor Turner Wright's pedigreed pigs. Since I was not on State's Discipline Committee in those days, I had only heard the campus gossip and not the true version of the escapade. Thus time bares the truth.

The plaque, which names the Volstorff Ballroom in the Student Union for her 41 years of service to SDSU Students. (J.O. Pedersen photo)

The 1935 football team, which beat the University of Wisconsin Badgers 13-6. (1936 Jack Rabbit photo)

Orlin E. Walder, dancing with Dean Volstroff at the opening of the new Student Union in 1973. "Prof." Walder served SDSU as Dean of Men and Director of Student Activities from 1935 to 1971. (University Relations photo)

I came to this campus in the fall of 1932, nearly seven decades ago, and half of the history of South Dakota State University. As I am now into my tenth decade of life, it seems a most appropriate time to take a look back at some of the traditions and shared memories of our University, mostly our sense of community and history.

I worked with eight College Presidents, forty-one Students' Association Presidents, including three women, and attended thousands of hours of Monday night Board of Control Meetings (now called the Student Senate), with their confusion, frustration, smoke and occasional real progress. I have survived three Directors of Student Activities: Professor Robert Past, Professor E.R. Binnewies and Professor Orlin E. Walder, who gallantly suggested that I take on his duties as Director of Students when he retired as Dean of Men.

I survived the depression, dust storms, rationing and three wars, blizzards and torrid prairie heat, thousands of tornado threats, searing or chilling winds, failed Regents' raids to cripple our academic functions, and a student revolution in manners and morals with its disturbing drug culture. There was never a dull moment, except perhaps in some faculty committee meetings. As someone said, "Committees are bodies that keep minutes and waste hours."

I came to South Dakota from Northwestern University in Chicago, where Lake Michigan marked my days with its many faces, its chill, cutting winds and soft, moonlit nights when we strolled on the beach and rested briefly in a gazebo in a neighboring garden. The lake almost ended my existence one day during a reckless sailboat ride. But that's another story, one of many private memories of a section of the Northwestern University campus where now there are modern apartment complexes instead of mansions and buildings built on a landfill where once there was water.

I remember Lake Michigan on the day my journey to South Dakota began. A frigid, damp wind blew off the lake as I trudged along Michigan Avenue, hugging close to the display windows, on a cold, cloudy day in February 1932. Even the exquisite oriental rugs, beautiful ceramics fine jewelry and luxurious fur coats did not tempt me to loiter in the chill wind. The day matched my mood, wondering why I was on my way to interview for a position in South Dakota—a place certain to be much colder than this.

I turned off on Jackson Boulevard to meet Dean George Brown from South Dakota State College, where there was an open position for a Dean of Women. My friend, Mrs. Goodell at the American College Bureau, had insisted that I take the interview. Dean McGraw, the Dean of Women at Northwestern, under whom I had worked as preceptress of two different dormitories, reminded me that history professors were a dime a dozen and administrative positions paid higher salaries. I would enjoy being a Dean of Women, she insisted—an opinion I seriously doubted at the time. But those were difficult times financially, and positions were scarce.

Dean of the College and the Division of General Science as well as acting president during several periods, was also president for six months in 1940. In the 1932 Jack Rabbit, Dean Brown said, "The success of a college is measured largely by the success of its graduates. The graduates of the first half-century [of SDSC's history]...were earnest in purpose, possessing high ideals and a passion to obtain an education. Their success should be a challenge to all who enter the College after them." (Briggs Library photo)

I forgot about the cold outside at for at that instant I caught Dean Brown's warm, welcome and sparkling brown eyes.

He told me about State and many of its traditions. He prepared me for the robust use of a barrel stave for paddling obstreperous freshmen and about the nightshirt parade during Hobo Week. He also carefully outlined what he hoped a new Dean of Women could accomplish. I learned that the previous Dean had a kind of nervous breakdown because of the serious illness of her mother. Another Dean had died, but one was still on campus, serving as Head of the Art Department.

After meeting Dean Brown in Chicago, I was invited to Minneapolis for an interview with President Charles W. Pugsley.

That turned out to be quite an interview; first with President Pugsley, and later joined by his wife and son, Albert. I could manage each alone, but to please all three at the same time required all of my ingenuity. I

Charles W. Pugsley, SDSC president from 1923 to 1940. (Briggs Library photo)

have always been grateful to Albert for what I assume was a favorable recommendation, and Mrs. Pugsley proved to be a true friend. I heard from her regularly for many years until her eyesight failed. She was a charming, delightful hostess, who unselfishly worked hours and hours on special details to make the affairs at the President's home, now called Woodbine Cottage again, memorable occasions for both students and faculty.

There was a partial eclipse of the sun on my first trip to South Dakota. I wondered if it was an omen, but I am an optimist. On the morning of my arrival on the Chicago & North Western train at a dismally early hour, Dean Brown was at the station to greet me. With a twinkle in his eyes he introduced me to an elderly lady who was waiting for her daughter. Dean Brown had told her of my arrival, and while they waited together for the train, she had delineated all the desirable traits and qualities needed by a good Dean of Women: advanced degrees, well traveled, past forty years of age, and so on. She was more than astonished when I was introduced and seemed to have some difficulty with her false teeth as she tried to acknowledge the introduction. Of course she emphatically disagreed with Dean Brown's decision to employ me, just 25 years old at the time.

Professor Albert Harding, Professor of History from 1897 to 1930 and Head of the History Department from 1931 to 1944. (Briggs Library photo)

Later at a delicious breakfast in his home, Dean Brown's wife regaled his family with her description of an ideal Dean of Women and her subsequent shock at meeting me. Some months afterward, I was able to win her respect by agreeing to do some radio programs on international affairs, which she was responsible for planning. My first severe critic eventually became a friend.

I received a warmer welcome from Professor Albert Harding, Head of the History Department, who informed me that I would be the first Ph.D. to teach in his department. Only a true gentleman would think of complimenting a frightened young woman before she had even met her first class. I had been anxious to meet Professor Harding after hearing so much about him from Dr. West, a physician practicing in Elgin, Ill., who grew up in Brookings. I knew his two sons at Northwestern, and Dr. West had made a special visit to tell me about Professor Harding the day I was frantically packing my wardrobe trunk to come to Brookings. He gave me a letter of introduction to the Professor. He also gave me a good impression of Brookings as a community, which helped to bolster my morale.

Fall 1932

On my first morning at State, I toured the campus. On one of my first stops, I met Ada B. Caldwell, whom I had heard so much about. She had assisted the former Dean of Women and was now Head of the Art Department. I soon learned why everyone admired her. She gave her energies to developing the talents of her students, rather than spending her time painting, though she loved to paint when precious vacation periods offered her the opportunity.

Probably her most illustrious student was Harvey Dunn, and many of his paintings are now housed in the South Dakota Art Museum on campus. I vividly recall the first formal faculty tea the women students held in the dormitories. I had pressured the Home Economics students to help me prepare open-faced, decorated sandwiches and flowers on homemade fondant patties. At the tea, Miss Caldwell said, with tears in her eyes, "You will bring beauty into the lives of your women students." Of course, I adored her from that moment until illness forced her retirement in 1935.

I also vividly recall hearing the Campanile chime on my first morning at State. Still today, this musical tower instills in me the sense of State's purpose, tying the past with the present, the long-since graduated alumni with the freshmen taking their first classes. The Campanile casts

Harvey Dunn's portrait of Ada B. Caldwell, who assisted the Dean of Women before 1932 and was Art teacher and Head of Art Department from 1899 to 1935. (Briggs Library photo)

the spell of belonging. Charles L. Coughlin, a graduate of the class of 1909, gave the Campanile to his alma mater at a cost of $75,000 in 1929.

The Coughlin, Campanile, a 1929 gift of Briggs & Stratton industrialist, Charles L. Coughlin (Class of 1909). (Agricultural Heritage Museum photo)

Ever since, countless couples have sat on its steps in spring and autumn nights, sharing their innermost thoughts and dreams. Students and faculty have watched the Campanile shrouded in fog, snow, ice crystals. We've seen it silhouetted against the sky on a star-studded night.

Campus poets boast of the celestial effect of the Campanile in the autumn moonlight, or in mid-morning fall, stark against skies so fierce and so freshly laundered blue, or clouds so white and so brisk. My thoughts that first morning were far less poetic, but the Campanile did leave a lasting impression.

In my first days at State, President Pugsley protected me almost as a father from making too many early mistakes. I learned to share my problems and projects with him before presenting them to the Committee of Deans. Dean Brown was a scholar and philosopher. President Pugsley was a practical person with a tremendous vision of the role of State if the financial requirements could be met by the State Legislature—a problem still prominent in higher education in South Dakota. Both men gave me their support and friendship and sustained me on many occasions, when I faced the hurdles of my hyphenated role of Dean of Women and History Professor.

When I accepted the Dean position, I had insisted on teaching some history classes, just in case I did not succeed in the administrative tasks. During those depression years, many students had been in and out of college for financial reasons, and several were my age. I was worried about this, but President Pugsley assured me that having my Ph.D., along with my self-confident style, would help me in my relationships with the students. That fall, there were only four new members of the faculty. Because of financial pressure, the staff had been greatly reduced, and frankly most of them were old enough to be my parents. Interesting exceptions, were these two young bachelors.

The semiformal reception for freshmen in the fall of 1932 was held in the women's residence halls. I came out of my apartment in Wecota Hall dressed in a black satin formal with rhinestone straps. One quick look at the attire of the faculty sent me back to my room to grab the jacket belonging to the formal, before taking my place in the receiving line next to the Student President, Jerome Krzmarjick. The next day the student social chairman came over to see me and said that everyone was talking about my red sandals.

I learned promptly that people at State were interested in everything. Their comments did not imply criticism, just interest, and they loved to gossip. I decided to be very careful, lest I provide grist for the gossip mill, and insisted on student escorts with a different one for each social occasion. Through the years, I had hundreds of escorts. Every fall semester, shortly before Thanksgiving vacation, a freshman male invariably would

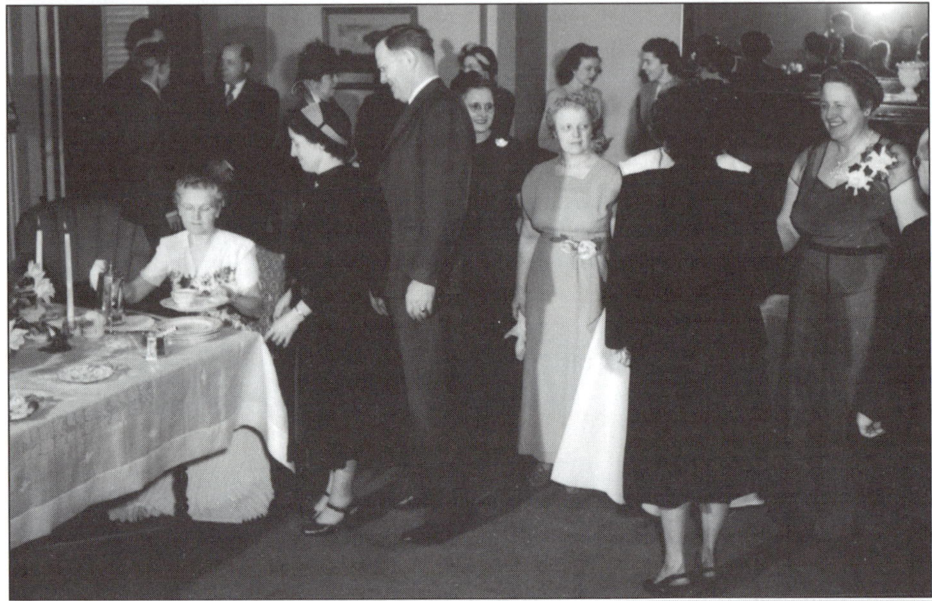

Reception for freshmen in the fall of 1932. (Vivian V. Volstorff photo)

come to my office, introduce himself and eventually ask, "Is it true that my Dad once took you to the Military Ball?" They all had been told by their parents to meet me and dared not go home without a visit.

In spite of my best efforts, it seemed inevitable for me to occasionally make a spectacle of myself those first few weeks. I just couldn't quite adjust to all of the new experiences, most memorable among them, the Hobo Week activities.

The only cultural program of the 1932 Hobo Week was Humperdinck's comic opera "Hansel and Gretel." It took place in the auditorium the night before the football game. My interest in the opera was interrupted when a strange young man kept looking at me. Dean Edith Pierson, who was with me, said, "He's a bootlegger! Don't pay any attention to him!" At first I was flabbergasted that she could identify him, but then I remembered that he owned the only new car on campus that year. In addition to being quite handsome, the nameless bootlegger was reputed to make deliveries to the door—whether in the dormitory or in town.

Float in the 1932 Hobo Day parade. (1933 Jack Rabbit photo)

The next morning before the Hobo Day parade, Dean Pierson made a pheasant brunch for the star of the opera, Constance Eberhardt from Evanston, and the director of the show. I marveled at Dean Pierson's energy and efficiency, since I was exhausted from a week of precious little sleep.

A few days later, President Pugsley convened a Board of Control meeting in his office to discuss the financial impacts of Hobo Week. It soon became obvious to him and everyone else assembled that I did not understand about the little houses that had been burned in a bonfire and for which the Board of Control must assume financial responsibility. The student president was too flustered to explain. Finally the editor of the *Collegian* passed a note to me and my face grew pink—a reaction fully appreciated by everyone present—at his explanation of an outhouse. Thus, I was initiated into rural life.

Prohibition was still the law my first year in Brookings, and there was little drinking on campus. Max Brown, a student leader, was reported to have unscrewed the tops of his mother's canned grape juice to tamper with the contents. There were no manuals back then on winemaking, and

I heard rumors that he had attached balloons to the jars. The truth came out when a jar exploded during a Sunday dinner.

My salary that year was $2,200.00 for twelve months. The rate for student labor varied from fifteen to twenty-five cents an hour, depending on whether they worked at the dormitory or switchboard or were a laboratory assistant. Room rent was $13.50 per quarter, and even an athlete could scarcely spend more than twenty to twenty-five cents for a good meal in the Wecota Cafeteria under Miss Louise Williams' management. Tuition was $24.00 a quarter with unlimited credit hours for resident students and $36.00 for nonresident students. Fees were simple: $3.50 for Student Activities, $1.00 for library usage, and $2.50 for health care. The School of Agriculture students (Aggies), generally older rural youth who did not finish high school, received agricultural and homemaking training for $50.00 for five months. In 1932, State's fall enrollment consisted of 951 students, with 837 in college, 93 Aggies and 23 special students. The male-female ratio was close to 4 to 1.

EARLY DAYS AT STATE

Finances were tight. To save money I used our part-time houseboy as a secretary, thereby alarming the entire community when his deep, masculine voice answered the telephone, "This is the Dean of Women's Office." Male students cut each other's hair, and there were some strange styles in order to save money for a Saturday night date. Only about a dozen students had cars on campus, and they definitely were not the envy of the faculty as they are today.

The early thirties students had to work in order to be in college. One young student, Dennis Moe, arrived on campus with exactly one dollar. A sympathetic Dr. Thomas Olson, head of the Dairy Department, loaned him fifty dollars. Dennis Moe earned a Bachelors and Masters degree from State and later an Honorary Doctorate from Augustana. He served twenty-six years as head of State's Agricultural Engineering Department.

During college, he earned six dollars a month, the maximum, for dusting under 24 typewriters and sweeping the floor on the second floor of Old North. This paid for his room, bed linens and the privilege of a single electric plate. His "refrigerator" was the space between the window and the storm sash. He also worked nights at the Rainbow Cafe for twenty cents an hour, and tips were rare. During Hobo Week, he worked until midnight every night and during every non-class period of the day.

The faculty was also tested hard. The total appropriation for operating State College for the 1933-1935 biennial period was $462,500—considerably less than the appropriation for the 1925-26 period. The cutbacks necessitated drastic reductions in salary and dismissals of surplus faculty. There was a report on campus that President Pugsley's $7,000.00 salary was reduced to $3,700.00, because he wanted the money given to faculty to keep them here. So many excellent and loyal professors received so little for their salaries in those depression days.

Many of my students asked me for emergency loans, but my own income was too meager to help them, because I was repaying loans I had made to complete my graduate work. I prevailed upon the Faculty Women's Club to allow me twenty-five dollars as an emergency loan fund. Students signed a note and

Dennis Moe, Head of Agricultural Engineering for 26 years from 1956 to 1982. (Instructional Technologies Center photo)

were charged no interest. The money was used for train or bus fares when family emergencies occurred, for meals for Indian students whose scholarship checks were late, for medications that were imperative for students' health, and when the expected one dollar did not come from home in a weekly laundry kit. Some students were too proud to confess their plight, and roommates or friends would tell me. I had jurisdiction over the fund for more than thirty years, and we never lost a cent. Never has so small a fund helped so many. With better economic conditions in the 1960s, I finally returned the twenty-five dollars back to the Faculty Women's Club.

Even for business owners, borrowing more than $500 in those days was considered outlandish. There were near riots in this period of farm foreclosures as relatives and friends attempted to control auctions by bidding pennies and nickels. Twenty-five cents could buy a dressed chicken or a three-pound loaf of bread. Sirloin steak was twenty-five cents a

Students worked in labs for twenty to twenty-five cents per hour. (Jack Rabbit photo)

pound. Wheat selling for $1.80 a bushel in 1920 brought thirty-eight cents in 1932; corn fell from sixty-one cents to thirty-two; and cotton from sixteen cents a pound to six. Prices were even lower as the drought and depression lingered.

Attending a student convention in Mitchell, South Dakota, in November of 1933, I discovered that Dakota Wesleyan paid its faculty partly in vouchers, which could be used to purchase items in the city. Eugene Vesey, a Northwestern graduate, was teaching English there, and he persuaded me to help him purchase some lingerie gifts for his mother and sister for Christmas. Assisting him with his shopping, I consoled myself with the thought that at least I worked at a state-supported college, where we were paid in money.

The living rooms in Wenona and Wecota Halls were shabby and sad looking, with furniture purchased in 1890.

The student rooms had a bare bulb, casting its glare from a cord in the center of the ceiling. After a few months on campus, I couldn't bear the drab surroundings any longer, so, in spite of the college's tight finances, I went to President Pugsley to ask him to pay for new furniture.

"I am sure that you have scientifically equipped labs, but there is nothing provided for social activities in the residence halls," I said. "The furnishings are badly worn and pathetically dull."

He looked at me and said, "Young lady, why do you think I hired you?"

With his blessing and a letter of introduction, I went to the Chicago Furniture Mart and selected furniture in the summer of 1933. Lester

Wecota Hall, built in 1917. (1937 Jack Rabbit photo)

Hienscheimer, the owner of the former Home Furniture Store in Sioux Falls, offered the thinnest margin to allow me to obtain the exact prices and fabrics I wanted through the bidding process. I had haunted his store, looking at furniture before my Chicago excursion, and he felt sorry for my furniture problems and me.

The store's interior decorator, Ms. Hult, helped me to identify furniture that was aesthetically attractive and sturdy enough to hold up under football players. The resulting pieces were of Elizabethan style, with lamps of opaque glass and silk shades of soft colors, accompanied by aqua wall-to-wall carpeting and rose draperies.

The carpeting, I recall, was in such good condition thirty years later when it was removed from the residence halls in the early '70s, it was reinstalled in the Dean of Student Service's office in the Administration Building.

One of my primary concerns about the new furniture was the likelihood of damage from students who smoked. There was a no smoking rule in the residence halls until Dr. Fred Leinbach, a pipe smoker, came in the late forties. A regulation abolishing smoking on campus of any of the institutions under Regents' control was passed on December 5, 1913, and is still on the books as far as I know. It reads: "Resolved, by the Regents of Education, that smoking of tobacco on the main campus of the University around the outside buildings, upon approaches to and in the corridors of buildings, in recitation and public assembly rooms, is forbidden." The veterans returning at the end of World War II flagrantly violated the rule. It was an almost impossible rule to enforce, and I was fearful of creating fire hazards if students tried stealthily dousing their cigarettes to avoid detection.

The dormitory regulations also required lights out at 11 p.m. and 11:30 p.m. for seniors on weekends. Overnight stays out of town, which I granted sparingly, were the subjects of critical action by the Committee of Deans in January of 1933. Out-of-town permissions were frankly frowned upon as dangerous. A couple of years before I retired, Dean Walder and I were going over some Board of Control changes, when Dean of Academic Affairs, Harold Bailey, came into my office and asked us if we had heard of the action of the Administrative Council. Then he read a statement about overnight stays that left Dean Walder and me in complete astonishment! Dean Bailey, with his eyes twinkling, grinned and gave the date of the proclamation: January 20, 1933. He had been cleaning out some of his inherited files.

My own ventures off campus in those first months were not without some confusion. With the exception of the names Medary and Main, all streets and avenues in Brookings were numbered and at right angles to one another. Thus, there was a first avenue along with a first street. I learned this fact the hard way.

Soon after my arrival at State, I was invited to a Kensington at five o'clock one afternoon. I assumed that a Kensington was a tea and that the hostess had planned it for an hour convenient for those who had to work until five. I did not have a car that first year (nor the second) and I went to the wrong address—on an avenue instead of a street. A harried looking housewife with her hair in pin curls answered the doorbell. I did not know her, and it was quite obvious that she was not giving a tea party. When I finally arrived, very late, at the correct street address, I discovered that a Kensington was a two-course supper party, followed by bridge until nine o'clock.

Much about Brookings has changed since 1932, but it can still be a difficult town in which to find a party. Today, with all the new additions like Indian Hills, Camelot Square, Hunters Ridge and the numerous cul-de-sacs and street names like Dogwood Avenue, Half-Moon Road,

An aerial view of the SDSC campus in the early '30s. (Briggs Library photo)

Lincoln Lane, Mustang Pass and Teton Lane, it is easy to get lost again in Brookings. Twenty-first Avenue South is in two unrelated pieces, and if you start out on First Street you may find yourself on Olwien, especially if it is a foggy or snowy night, and you are not acquainted with the area.

The campus has changed as well. In 1932 there were about 22 buildings and structures on campus.

Two buildings burned down, Agricultural Engineering and Development Hall. Several others have been razed: Old North, Old Central, Music Hall, Extension Building, East Men's Hall, an Economics Building, Wildlife Building, Dairy Building and the Storehouse. New dairy units and a storehouse have been built at the north end of the campus. The Music Department is now housed in Lincoln Hall, formerly the library, with a lovely concert hall and soundproof practice rooms.

Today the campus is a mixture of old, classic structures like the 1912 Administration Building with its marble interior walls, the 165-foot-tall Campanile and the Sylvan Theater, and modern more recent facilities like the Animal Science Building, Rotunda, Briggs Library, New University Union, the Stan Marshall Health, Physical Education and Recreation Center and the Northern Plains Bio-Stress Center. By the end of the century the SDSU campus includes 119 academic buildings with a replacement value of $182,606,251, plus 31 revenue buildings with a replacement value of $72,116,933.

Old North and the clock tower in the early '30s. The clock, donated by the Classes of '22 and '23, marked the time for all students. (1933 Jack Rabbit photo)

Accreditation teams have commented about the beauty of our campus, its flowers, well-kept look, and lack of graffiti. There are two Greek fraternity residences located on the eastern edge of the campus: Farm House and Alpha Gamma Rho, built on land acquired from the University for a nominal cost. On Eighth Street, just south of Harding Hall, the former Professor Olson's house is now the Chi Omega and Prof.

Old North clock tower is now located in the Tompkins Alumni Plaza. Original Old North Clock still helps students keep track of the time. (Instructional Technologies Center photo)

Lundy's house is the Alpha Xi Delta house. The greatest growth in new buildings occurred since 1960, most of them under the regime of President Hilton Briggs.

The Victory Bell, dear to the hearts of many alumni who recall its ringing whenever the athletic teams won, now has its own bell tower on the brick patio of the Tompkins Alumni Center. Nearby is another piece of State memorabilia, the Old North Clock, the campus timepiece that was saved when the Old North structure was demolished.

But many of my strongest memories of those early days at State have no physical memorial. On Armistice Day in 1933 came the great Black Blizzard. The dust storm was a wall of wind and dirt so thick it turned daylight into pitch darkness. Soil drifted into the Wecota Hall sunroom several inches thick and the wind tore off part of the tar-paper roof. Dirt engulfed fences, choked cattle and humans, and even destroyed car windshields. It was a day and night of desolation.

I felt like departing immediately. But South Dakota residents had lived through more than a decade of bad weather and poor crops and took it in stride. I thought the land had gone berserk! Streetlights had to be turned on at midday.

The countryside became eerie, as I'd see a dark mass converging in the distance. Blondes, brunettes and redheads all looked the same when they were caught in a dust storm at a track meet. Crops and soil were lost, and animals suffered along with human beings. Janitors and maids were distressed by the magnitude of their cleaning chores. The dirt was endless and everywhere. I tasted it, felt its grit, smelled its dryness and blinked it from my eyes. The brown bareness of the scenery was overwhelming, and I wanted to go home.

Streetlights are on at 3:00 p.m. in Watertown during the Dust Bowl Days. (Agricultural Heritage Museum photo)

We all have scars from the dust bowl period that I am sure it will always be a part of us. (Mine is continued sinus infections.)

But just as I was about to give up on my State assignment, I learned I was already considered by others to be a permanent fixture. The first summer school reception I attended was held in the women's dormitories. After the receiving line disbanded and refreshments were served, the guests were seated in the sunroom for a program by Dr. Ward Miller, Professor of Botany, who was to entertain two generations of State students with his magic and marvelous ad libbing patter. On this occasion, he was setting up a large easel and remarking to the audience that we did not know he was also an able portrait painter.

"Many of you know this person, and all of you will after tonight," he said, swinging the easel around to face the audience. The portrait it displayed was of me!

I let out an astonished, "You Bum!"

"I have been called many names," he replied, "but so help me, never before have I been called a bum in public at a reception by a Dean of Women. It is certainly not a fitting term for my considerable artistic talent."

Dr. Ward Miller, Professor of Botany, from 1928 to 1969, entertained several gener-ations of State students with his magic and marvelous ad libbing. (Instructional Technologies Center photo)

By this time the audience was convulsed with laughter and my coun-tenance had gone from pink to scarlet. I had remembered how my friend, Mabel Browner, had asked for a picture of me for her eight-year old son, Ron, to use at school for some kind of show and tell. It was the sudden knowledge of the devious way that Dr. Miller had obtained my picture that had caused my outburst.

After the show, Dr. Miller explained that he had taken a picture of my picture, enlarged it and painted over it with magical fluids. Another con-coction applied at the reception removed the paint to reveal my photo-graph, much to my chagrin and to the grins of my students.

Lest anyone believe that Dr. Miller and I were at odds over this episode, let me hasten to explain that he assisted me many years in demonstrations for my notorious freshmen lectures. Since he was three-

Typical college coeds, glasses and all. (1933 Jack Rabbit photo)

fourths of my height and about half of my width, our demonstrations on correct dancing positions and the like, with some slight exaggerations on our part, were remembered, when mere words would have been readily forgotten.

In my early days at State, there were no slacks, shorts, wigs or elaborate cosmetics, except mascara. Eye shadow was used only for stage makeup. Hair dye and tints were only used by women of ill repute. Everyone wore baggy rayon hose, which twisted around our legs like barber poles. Nylon hose were just beginning to be used when the supply was taken for parachutes prior to World War II. Silk stockings, which were costly, were saved for dates and special dress-up affairs. In class, coeds wore Bobbie socks and saddle shoes, skirts and sweaters or blouses. Their skirts covered their knees and a generous part of their legs. Girls had their hair marcelled with a marcelling iron. They nearly always wore hats. A favorite was a tam, which looked like a beret with a pom pom on top. Girls were lucky to have two good dresses and a simple formal. They came with a steamer trunk in the fall and sent it home in the spring by train. For male students, hair was neatly cut with a straight part. A boy might slicker his hair with pomade if it was windy outside or if he just liked the slick look. Suits were worn, or if he was feeling pretty casual, he would wear trousers with a jacket or sweater. It was long before designer denims became a fad.

Coeds stole illicit puffs of cigarettes in their rooms, as the most daring thing they could think of doing, sometimes hanging their heads out of windows to prevent the smoke from being detected. Through one of the many government alphabet projects of the Roosevelt period, mature women came to State for summer school, which helped them train for positions as cooks and the like. As a part of this routine, they dressed in shorts and walked across campus for their calisthenics in mid-afternoon, much to the consternation of the janitors and secretaries. Even the students disapproved of this activity and thought the women looked terrible. They were not good figures, but ample, mature ones with all sorts of bulges. By today's standards, their dress was almost modest, but in those days, no women's knees were seen in public.

There also were no laundromats. For some students, the event of the week was a letter from mother with a dollar bill enclosed in the canvas laundry bag. The mailman was almost over-run by students when he brought the laundry bags, because everyone was hoping that some goodies were enclosed. The trick was to get your laundry bag to your room to explore it without your friends seeing it. Though the treats were eventually shared with roommates, all students hoped to have privacy while opening their kits.

Student activities were fun, many were free, and some were creative pranks. I often found myself the object of the latter. One pair thought it would be fun to borrow some white rats from the Experiment Station to be let loose in the Wecota parlor just at dusk, so that I would be certain to see them when I turned on the lights. David Hume, the freshman in the white rat episode, was honored as a distinguished alumnus shortly before he retired from government service. His partner in the prank, who had access to the research rats, was Oscar Olson. He later became Dean of the Graduate School, and State's BioChemistry labs are named after him.

In the residence halls, there were no room telephones, no self-regulatory hours, no unsupervised coed areas, no visitations and no beer or refrigerators in which to put it. There were no student members of the Board of Regents, no TVs or sophisticated computers, and certainly no efforts by the students to evaluate the faculty or their tenure. There were no drug busts or street crime. Pregnancy and shoplifting cases, though very rare, were serious counseling matters because those were the days of when the University had stewardship over student behavior. (This was called *in loco parentis*).

I have carried suitcases of stolen merchandise back to the merchants to prevent a college co-ed from having a police record. Until 1950, I escaped being on the Discipline Committee because I insisted that serving on that committee would harm my role as a counselor. The dual role of history professor and dean helped me. During the first meeting of each

Oscar Olson and roommate Linus Werner in front of East Men's Hall. (Elaine (Mrs. Oscar) Olson photo)

Dr. Oscar Olson, Head of Biochemistry from 1952 to 1973 and Dean of the Graduate School from 1958 to 1965. (Industrial Technologies Center photo)

class every year, I always told my new students: "The Dean of Women never comes into the history classroom."

Crime of a more violent nature was rare in those days. I do recall the stir caused by the most famous criminal event in Brookings, and the lucky young journalist who was there to photograph it. Rarely does a photographer have the chance to be at the scene of a robbery with a loaded camera. At 11:00 a.m. on October 31, 1938, a State student, Woodrow Wentzy, photographed the robbery of the Northwest Security National Bank of Brookings. The site of this notorious bank robbery later became the Ram Pub in 1973. Woody was visiting with a friend in front of Kendall's Drug when the alarm went off. He took two photos: one of the couple fleeing to their getaway car and another of the car as it sped off.

The robbers took a hostage and headed north on Medary Avenue to old U.S. 77. By the old golf course north of town they stopped and threw carpenter tacks over the road. The tactic apparently worked.

After witnessing the getaway, Wentzy bought some flash bulbs at Kendall's drug store so he could take photographs inside the bank. He got shots of the open vault and stunned bank employees with a total of four negatives. The Sioux City Journal used his picture of the open vault, but neither of the getaway photos made the story because they were blurred. He received good coverage from the event, getting a byline and twenty-five dollars for his efforts.

The crime was originally thought to be the work of gangster Pretty Boy Floyd, but Ben and Stella Mae Dickson were convicted of the crime and an August 25, 1938, robbery of the Corn Exchange Bank in Elkton, S.D.

Exciting times, those early days of mine at State.

SURVIVING IN THE THIRTIES

ENTERTAINING ACTIVITIES

A University is supposed to sow generously the seeds of knowledge in students. Most students, however, spend at least a fraction of their time sowing the seeds of mischief. I prefer the wholesome, ingenious mischief of the past to the present escapism, via the drug culture and malicious hooliganism.

I didn't personally witness a few of my favorite stories of these long-forgotten shenanigans, as they occurred before I arrived at State. But, knowing how much I enjoyed a good tale, the late Professor Roy (Jake) Herold shared with me these four cases, and I now share them with you.

The Norwegian Independence Day, May 17th, was at hand. A few of the boys with Nordic heritage decided to mark the occasion for all of the student body. They settled on a firecracker composed of 10 blocks of nitroglycerin as a fitting tribute to their homeland. The trouble began when the firecracker creators did not realize that nitroglycerin blocks came in two strengths—one eight times stronger than the other—and they unknowingly secured the stronger of the two. Therefore, the ten blocks when assembled were 80 times stronger than anticipated.

Shortly before midnight, the boys placed the super cracker in the middle of campus, between the Administration Building and Wecota Hall, and hid themselves and their detonator in a small clump of trees not far away. At the stroke of 12 o'clock, one of the boys pushed the plunger, and the whole group was immediately thrown backward by the force of the blast. When the dust settled, the hole in the earth was quite evident, and all lights in the dorms were on. There were even reports of windows broken in the Administration Building. But the firecracker pranksters did not stay to see the damage. They were seen leaving the campus on a north route, most likely because the night watchman was coming up from the south and all the houses on the south side of Ninth Street were lit up.

Old East Men's Hall overlooked the practice cottage, where Home Economics classes were taught.

East Men's Hall was constructed in 1921 and torn down in 1976. The Tompkins Alumni Center and the Alvilda Myre Sorensen Center are now located on that site. (Agricultural Heritage Museum photo)

Two of the most congenial students on campus lived on the second floor of Old East facing the cottage. One day, the Dean of Home Economics was personally instructing a cooking class, and she placed a pot of pudding with a wooden handle out on the porch to cool. The two students, tempted by the aromas and being of an ingenious nature, got out a fishing rod and attached a weight and triple hook to the line. They lowered the hook and by swinging the line were able to snag the bail of the kettle and carefully reel it in. They reported later that the pudding was excellent but could not compare with the thrill of seeing the astonished expression on the Dean's face when she came out to retrieve her kettle.

Hobo Day, as always, was good for humor. On this particular occasion, two male students decided to costume themselves as a boy and his date. The date happened to be a very small boned man with a tenor voice. Two of the dorm girls found him clothes and shoes, and with a little padding here and there, he fit the part well.

After a long walk from the college to downtown, the impersonator suggested they step into a cigar store so he could rest his feet because his heels hurt. A USD student who had been drinking moonshine sidled up to the impersonator and put his arm around him. The impersonator pushed him away and moved closer to his accompanying friend. But the admirer was not so easily dissuaded. As he again leaned into the impersonator, he was quickly met by a punch in a chin—thrown by the "woman." He fell to the floor as the impersonator and his friend began to leave, only to hear the following comment from the out-of-towner: "My god, what a co-ed! I'm glad I don't go to this college." The other thing he didn't know about the "co-ed" was that "she" was a bantam-weight fighter.

The 1935-36 ROTC Regimental Staff—Back Row: Diehl, Vick, Leach, Jurens, Richeer, Axford, Olson; Front Row: Emmerich, Steele, Able, Sundet, Spicer, Sisson, Walz, Phelps. (1936 Jack Rabbit photo)

On another occasion, the Reserve Officer Training Corps (ROTC) was scheduled to exhibit its mighty military power. To allow for a full demonstration of all weapons, a sandbag wall was erected on the north end of campus to collect the machine gun fire and mortar. The night before the exhibition, it rained quite hard, and the sandbags became soaked and solid.

The next morning, the machine gunner took his demonstration position and fired one burst and then a second. As he was preparing for his third round, a man came running out of the old stock pavilion shouting, "Stop, stop!" The first round had cut a hole through the sandbags, and the second round had ventilated the stock pavilion roof.

With the machine gun demonstration unexpectedly over, the cadets hurried to prepare the exhibition of mortar fire. Distance of the shots was regulated by the number of small packets or rings of powder placed on the end of the projectile. In all of the excitement, the two cadets preparing the demonstration were a bit confused and they put two extra rings in place. They dropped in the projectile and covered their ears from the tremendous explosion. The projectile soared away, crossed Ninth Street and dropped through an old garage roof. It was a beautiful exhibition, but one not appreciated by the Professor of Military Science and Tactics!

Hearing these historic stories was some small relief for me, as I had worried that all the pranksterism started with my arrival at State. During those early years, the tricks came fast and furious, but they also made my new home a great deal of fun.

One late evening, I discovered a calf in the Wecota Hall lobby. Being raised a city girl, I had no idea how to herd the animal outside. As instructed, I placed a call to the power plant to ask for assistance from the night watchman, of which there was only one on duty. The power plant blinked the lights of the hall to summon the night watchman, and I waited as the calf stalked the lobby, looking for its mother.

I waited and waited and waited. When the night watchman showed up an hour later, he asked, "Where's the cat I'm supposed to put out?" I indignantly explained that it was a calf, not a cat, and that I already had enlisted the help of a female student with a 4-H background in removing the animal for me.

My suspicion was that the night watchman was slow in responding to the request because I frequently violated the lights-out regulation, staying up late to prepare lectures and speeches. He invariably would ring the doorbell to ask if everything was all right. Even though I explained each time that I was a night person who could not concentrate until the dorms were quiet, he was objecting instinctively to my disobedience of the rules.

That wasn't my only experience with cattle in the dormitory. Early in my career I learned that you could make a cow climb up stairs, several flights in fact, but no amount of coaxing would persuade her to come

Bill Blegan with animated lawn mower for Prof. MacDougal's lawn. (Vivian V. Volstorff photo)

down the steps. I recruited a posse of male students to slide her down on her side on blankets while I looked on in extreme discomfort, distaste and frustration. I could call a maintenance man at night if a pipe broke in order not to flood the cafeteria, but I dared not call one to clean up after a nervous cow. Dean Brown had not prepared me for this experience! But, thankfully, I wasn't the only one the student pranksters targeted.

During Senior Week, a group of senior engineers led by Bill Blagen arranged to borrow some goats from the eccentric owner of a very shabby looking place, where Harding Hall stands today. They painted signs reading, "Animated lawn mowers," hung them around the necks of the goats and then staked the animals in Professor Herbert MacDougal's yard on

Medary Avenue. He was a popular professor of Mathematics who had become somewhat neglectful in trimming his lawn after the birth of twin sons.

The next morning at 6:30 a.m., Bill called Professor MacDougal on the phone, and while he was talking, the other seniors rescued the goats. I knew of the scheme because the boys told me of their plans in minute detail and even invited me to participate, an offer I declined. Later that day when I entered the Administration Building to teach a history class, I saw Mac and asked sweetly, "How did you like the goats?"

"What do you know about them?" Mac demanded.

But all I said was, "Plenty," as I hurried off to class.

The same lads once before hid a pal's car engine, carefully wrapped in oilcloth, in the shrubbery by my apartment for a whole week. Imagine the owner's surprise when he lifted the lid of his car! In spite of his being a prankster, Bill was honored several years ago, deservedly so, as a distinguished engineer.

There was no union or center for student activities prior to 1940 when Pugsley Student Union opened. It was no wonder that students were searching for entertaining activities in the '30s. Eventually, I persuaded several faculty families to invite small groups of students into their homes on Sunday evenings for forum discussions. Someone would read an article in the *Atlantic Monthly*, the *New York Times* or some comparable publication. (I was accused of starting a *New York Times* cult in Brookings.) Professor and Mrs. Tom Olson hosted such group discussions for several years.

There were no church youth centers or directors in 1932, but the YMCA and YWCA organizations flourished and presented excellent programs until they became victims of the lack of funding available during World War II.

I started the tradition of a Saturday Matinee Tea Dance for the seniors during Senior Week, a week of vacation prior to graduation. This tradition lasted as long as the senior vacation remained on the College Calendar.

For me, the name of a senior football player will be forever associated with that first tea dance. It was another open house where it seemed as though I didn't know a soul. I introduced myself to the first student I could find and said I did not know his name. When he told me it was Uno, I apologized for being so stupid.

"Uno Strong, of course, the football player," I said.

YMCA and YWCA organizations were the only organizations intended to further religious life on campus in the '30s. (1939 Jack Rabbit photo)

Later at the Military Ball, I was experiencing some difficulty dancing with Uno. I could not move my right foot at times. He was getting hot and annoyed, and I was perplexed until I looked down and saw the lining of my dancing sandal extending several inches out of the toe. He kept stepping on it, so that I could not move. I pulled the lining out and thoroughly enjoyed the rest of the dance but wondered if Uno would ever care to encounter me again.

That question was answered when Uno brought the entire senior football squad to the first matinee dance I organized. To please me, they nibbled away daintily and the open-faced sandwiches and petit cakes and then politely asked the senior women to dance.

From the fall of 1932 until my retirement in 1973, the Sigma Lambda Sigma members assisted me with informal fireside cozies for freshman women and new transfers.

I called them cozies rather than teas, in order to keep them informal. They were held in Wenona lounge with a pleasant fire going in the fireplace. The food was good, as I sat up most of the night making sandwich rolls for my guests, serving from 2 to 6 p.m. to accommodate the students' schedules. The cozies served three purposes: (1) to enable the freshman and transfer women, both those who lived in town and those in

Sigma Lambda Sigma members assist with 'fireside cozy teas' for freshman women. (Vivian V. Volstorff photo)

the dormitory, to get acquainted; (2) to allow them to get to know me as an individual in a comfortable setting, so that there would be no barrier when they needed counseling; and (3) to develop in them, I hoped, some social graces, which I felt were very important for educated women. The Sigma members each had a list of freshman and transfer women whom they invited and subsequently acted as unpaid counselors to their group—a fitting program for a senior honor organization based on leadership, scholarship and service.

At my first cozy, a young woman from the West River country looked rather contemptuously at the plate of lemon and orange wedges, some laced with whole cloves, and a mound of crystalline ginger.

I noticed her upturned nose and asked innocently, "Well, what would you prefer in your tea, then?"

"I'll take mine straight," she replied.

I must hasten to add that I remember that this student, as a junior, won an honorarium of $500 for an article she'd written about horses, which was published in an Eastern journal. That was a lot of money in the mid-thirties. It could buy a new four-door Ford. I know, because I had to wait several years before I had enough money of my own to buy one.

An innocent comment of mine at a winter Board of Control meeting one night during my first year at State gave birth to the Rabbit Rarities. I consider this to be a somewhat dubious honor. Money was scarce at the time, too scarce to import talent, and I suggested that there was a lot of talent on campus. Talent that included members of student dance bands, the engineers' bottle band, a host of talented musicians and drama students, and lads like David Hume who could impersonate any member of the faculty at a moment's notice. So, I suggested they start an all college talent show, using the WAA Mu show at Northwestern University as an example. I explained that spin-offs from this show became professional productions like "Clara, Lu and Em," which was radio's first daytime serial. It featured three former Northwestern coeds, Louise Starkey Mead as Clara, Helen King Mitchell as Em and Isobel Carothers Berolzheimer as Lu. I mentioned that Louise Starkey was getting a salary of $18,000 a year in 1932. I had ridden a train with her back to Evanston during my struggle to finish my dissertation in the summer of 1932.

The idea of Rabbit Rarities flourished, although never well done according to the present day standards of the speech and drama department.

The shows were fun and usually sponsored by the Board of Control. Once during the petticoat rule of World War II, the *Collegian* staff sponsored the show when Evangeline Anderson was editor. Again in the winter of 1939 the State band sponsored the show to help raise funds for their trip to Winnipeg, Canada, where they later played at the Royal Welcome Week ceremonies for King George VI of Great Britain and his Queen Elizabeth. The show has now disappeared from our campus activities and was replaced in the early 1960s by Capers, a production much more anemic than Rabbit Rarities but of far better quality. Capers, which originally started as a talent show called Cottontail Capers produced by freshmen during freshman week, was later sponsored by Alpha Psi Omega, a professional dramatics honor society, and frequently featured a theme and elaborate scenery.

Twice that I remember, the students coaxed me into participating in Rabbit Rarities. I played in a skit entitled, "The Shaming of Dan

Rabbit Rarities shows were rare, fun and usually sponsored by the Board of Control. (1940 Jack Rabbit photo)

McGrew," a weird take-off on Shakespeare, with Earl James, the professor who headed dramatics. It was a ridiculous script, at one point requiring me to bounce the professor on my lap. I should add he was of a delicate stature.

Years later, a group of Blue Key members, who were sponsoring the show, talked me into dancing the Charleston with a football player, Beverly Craig, who was an excellent dancer and in fine physical condition. I tried to refuse, but they already had the president's approval and that of Mrs. Lucille Dory, a regent. Both thought it would be good public relations! I was a little shaken by the audacity of the president and a regent volunteering my services for such a dubious performance, but I reluctantly agreed to help out.

The show was put on for several nights. I have talked from the same auditorium platform many, many times at freshmen lectures, but my knees shook violently as I waited in the wings that first night. Halfway across the stage, I heard a roar of recognition. My dance partner, by the

Dean Volstorff dancing the Charleston with Beverly Craig at the '39 Rabbit Rarities. (1940 Jack Rabbit photo)

way, became Creator/CEO of the World Dairy Expo., Inc., and lived in Madison, Wis.

Many years later, Jim Klassen, formerly on the Brookings High School faculty, told a radio audience on a Saturday morning about meeting my Charleston dancing partner. My students who were listening could scarcely believe their ears. I received some kidding, particularly from my class on Contemporary Europe. I had not heard the radio program, but Jim finally called me and confessed that he had mentioned Beverly Craig on his radio program.

Robert Jones, the son of a professor, was manager of Rabbit Rarities when one act consisted of two football teams, each member labeled with the name of a faculty person. The students ingeniously mimicked the professional mannerisms and idiosyncrasies in a highly exaggerated fashion. It was hilarious fun, but I was afraid heads would roll. Fortunately, the faculty took the act in stride, doubtless because so many were involved. Besides, during the depression, we needed hearty laughter.

Robert Knutson, the mid-'50s King of Comedy, who created the character "Obert Nutson". (1954 Jack Rabbit photo)

Student pranks continued into the '50s. It was April Fool's Day, during a spring snowstorm in the early '50s, and the hammer and sickle flag of the Soviet Union flew atop the Campanile. Orlin Walder, Dean of Men, received several telephone calls telling him about the flag, but he laughed at them, thinking the calls were pranks. Finally, when Melvin Henrichsen's wife, who helped Mel manage East Men's Hall, called him, he decided to venture out in the storm to investigate. Meanwhile, Harlan Olson, manager of Pugsley Union, had also received several complaints about the Soviet flag. Harlan, aghast at such a sacrilege, bounded through the snow and up the stairs of the Campanile to remove the flag. He had it locked in his office safe by the time Dean Walder arrived at the scene.

Who can forget Robert Knutson, the mid-'50s King of Comedy, who created the character "Obert Nutson"? Bob was one of the best comedians to ever attend State.

SATURDAY NIGHTS

In the '30s, summer Saturday nights were the week's social event for many Brookings area residents. Saturday night was the time for shopping, for haircuts, and maybe a movie. Remarkable as it may seem, the biggest problem was parking. Parking was adequate as far as spaces were concerned, but the goal was to get a spot on Main Avenue, preferably near the popular Taylor's corner or by the eating places, Bartelt's, Moriarty's, Nick's and the Tasty Shoppe. Taylor's corner specialized in chocolate sodas, as well as tobacco products and magazines. Four drug stores offered fountain service. Matson's, Tydball's, Ray's and Kendall's dispensed wonderful treats, such as double-dip cones, delicious sodas, chocolate malteds and lemon cakes. The soda fountain eventually went the way of the nickel ice cream cone. Now there are no drug stores on Main Avenue in Brookings.

At the time, there were no bars in town, because Brookings did not allow the sale of liquor until a citywide vote in 1955. Nearby Aurora was the place to go if you wanted to buy liquor. Other kinds of shopping, however, were favorite Saturday night activities. Afterward, the women would sit in their cars just watching the people or perhaps visiting with a neighbor. The younger children, reunited for a few hours with friends, ran up and down the street and through the alleys, all with dripping ice cream cones. The adolescents sought out their friends in Brookings, whose parents let them drive their Model Ts. They would dash out of town and then hurry back to Main Avenue—before they were missed, they hoped.

There were plenty of Model Ts in Brookings in the early thirties. Produced from 1909 to 1927, they rattled, vibrated and shook. The Model Ts started by crank, which required a considerable amount of choking and left the cars especially susceptible to stalling when climbing hills. Fortunately, the Brookings prairie area was flat. The intensity of the headlights depended on the speed of the car: The faster you went, the better the lights. But my engineering students assured me that this problem could be nicely overcome by simply driving in low gear. A slow car speed caused high engine speed, and thus, better lights. Plus, slow speed made for a more pleasant ride when a young man drove his best gal in the countryside on a summer evening.

I could not understand why this Saturday night scene was so attractive to the college students. They joined the street watchers regularly,

One of many Model T's in Brookings in the early thirties. (Agricultural Heritage Museum photo)

especially after the first picture show and until the curfew hours at the dormitories. Town people were just as avid fans of this street scene, perhaps because there was no cost involved and much gossip was exchanged.

Generally I avoided Main Avenue on Saturday nights, but one evening I reluctantly agreed to a trip up and down the street in the Fishback surrey, prior to the Ag barn dance. Hoping to conceal my identity, I borrowed a sunbonnet from Mrs. E.R. Binnewies, and pulled it tight around my face. No such luck.

"Hi, Dean Volstorff," came a lusty voice from the sidewalk. It was an insurance salesman whom I had repeatedly refused to date.

Later, when the college annual appeared in the spring, I saw that the surrey had a sign on the back reading, "Just Married."

BROOKINGS BUSINESS

Some Brookings family businesses have remained, most notably Nick's Hamburger Shop, which was started by Harold Niklason Sr., in 1929, in the building housing Reynolds Printing.

Nick's Hamburger Shop, was started by Harold Niklason in 1929 and still serves great hamburgers. (Agricultural Heritage Museum photo)

The business was moved to its present location, the familiar white stucco corner, in 1931. Nick's had a simple formula for success. Bypassing trendy atmosphere and fancy menus, Nick's sold hamburgers, plain and simple. Duane Larson bought the business from Harold Niklason, Jr. In 1977, National Public Radio named Nick's one of the top 82 burger eateries in the country.

Taylor's Corner became Logue's Corner and is now known as Ray's Corner. The pictures of the old tavern stand in stark contrast to the many younger, fast-paced bars in this University town. The long, dimly lit hall, scarcely over 12 feet wide, is covered with magazine racks and glass cases containing pipes and other tobacco products. The old tin ceiling that was once white is now yellow from decades of exposure to smoke-saturated air. On-tap beer has long since replaced the soda fountain, but the tavern's clientele remains the same. Groups of friends get together for a game of cards or a few beers.

Other local favorites have long since gone out of business. Mr. and Mrs. R. H. Bartelt, who operated the basement Coffee Shop, served delicious food to their devoted patrons of town and faculty. How we relished

It started as Taylor's Corner, became Logue's Corner and is now known as Ray's Corner. (Agricultural Heritage Museum photo)

her pastries and his superbly prepared meats, but that was more than fifty years ago!

Mr. and Mrs. John Moriarty started a restaurant in the Louis Johnson building, and after a decade they moved and enlarged their restaurant on the site of the Mulhair store, where it operated for 10 more years. By the end of that time, their children had finished college. John received a degree in Pharmacy; Cecilia a degree in Home Economics; Joseph a degree in Pharmacy, Medicine and Surgery; James a degree in Chemical Engineering, Medicine and Neurology, and Paul, a degree in Civil

Engineering. The entire family served the community with coffee and donuts, pie, Coca-Cola and soup, and took care of the late intermission dance crowds. Paul took charge of the popcorn machine, selling in front of the store and at band concerts in Pioneer Park during the summer. John and Paul kept up the business in Brookings with their mother. Until her death, "Grandma" Moriarty was never seen in public without one of her signature hats, and she still presided over her birthday parties in the Plaza Shopping Center, which John owned and operated. Paul started building homes, then apartments for rent and later commercial and industrial buildings.

In October 1982, Grandma Moriarty and two of her sons, John and Paul, were honored by the Brookings Area Chamber of Commerce for outstanding community service. The Moriartys were cited for their successful family real estate enterprise, which has helped Brookings grow, and for their good deeds in the community. At the ceremony, John Bibby, in presenting the award said: "They have invested their time, energy, talents and resources in their hometown."

This family certainly personified the local work ethic. Cecilia was lovely, and I am sure there were times when she and her brothers would have preferred to be with their peers, instead of serving their mother's home-made soup, chocolate cake and pies. However, they remained loyal to the family business.

Of all the family businesses operating in the 1930s, only three remain. They are Rude's Furniture, the Moriarty Company, and the Fishback bank, first called the Security National and now the First National Bank.

The story behind First National Bank is an interesting one, too. In North and South Dakota, economic stresses came in the 1920s, before the stock market crash, forcing the closing of many banks. Eighty percent of the North Dakota banks closed in the twenties. The stresses caused the closing of six banks out of eight in Sioux Falls. By the fall of 1925, two of the four banks in Brookings had already failed, a third had to be closed and reorganized, and the fourth closed later. It was in such a setting that the present First National Bank in Brookings began. A group of local citizens led by Horace Fishback, Sr., felt there was a need, and they had the courage to attempt a new banking operation. At the age of 68, Horace Fishback opened the Security National Bank on November 2, 1925. "Security" was a comforting title for a new bank in a depression.

The Security National is now the First National Bank, located at four different Brookings sites. Under the leadership of the Fishback family, the bank has become a regional financial service institution and includes several out of Brookings locations. (Agricultural Heritage Museum photo)

South Dakota lost more people during the depression than any other state in the upper Midwest. Between 1931 and 1941, the state lost 11.7 percent of its population. Many moved to California or Oregon. Per capita income for South Dakotans fell from $358 in 1930 to $129 in 1933. Between 1920 and 1934, 71 percent of the state's banks failed. State banks went from 557 in number to 148 during that period. National banks were reduced from 135 to 34. In 1936, the federal government estimated that wind erosion and drought had damaged 95 percent of the state's land.

Responding to the national troubles, South Dakota in 1932 did something highly uncharacteristic. It elected two liberal Democrats to Congress who backed Roosevelt's New Deal in Washington. Throughout the despair, changes were to come to the plains—tree shelter belts, electricity in the farm homes, and the federal government buying cattle, sheep and hogs from 67,000 state farmers who did not have the feed to sustain them. That represented 42 percent of South Dakota's livestock.

Students from farm homes came back in the autumn with bronzed skins, because they had supplemented the meager pasture with roadside grazing of the cattle. Day in and day out, along with the livestock, they breathed dust.

There were searing temperatures and hot, southwest winds, and the land continued to blow in the wind. Sometimes at night there would be

The impact of the depression and dust bowl caused more South Dakotans to leave the state than out-migrated from any other state in the Upper Midwest. (Agricultural Heritage Museum photo)

lightning, but it was heat lightning. Any youth growing up on a South Dakota farm in the '20s and '30s would not likely find anything particularly difficult in subsequent years. They were survivors.

On one of those very hot days, Dr. Pugsley called and asked me to please sit next to Rex Tugwell at a banquet in his honor at the former "Just a Mere" tea room. What I was not prepared for were the "down-to-earth" jokes of Governor Berry, South Dakota's cowboy governor from 1933 to 1937.

Rex Tugwell headed the Triple A (Agricultural Adjustment Administration), program. He was a very handsome man—suave, urban and utterly charming. His expertise greatly impressed me. The Triple A program made speedy headway. The farmer's cash earnings, thanks to higher prices and the AAA benefit payments, rose from four and a third billion dollars in 1932 to over seven in 1935.

President Pugsley, alert to the possibilities of the Works Progress Administration, acted immediately and paved the way for three new buildings on our campus: Wecota Annex, Scobey Hall (at first called West

Governor Berry, South Dakota's cowboy governor from 1933 to 1937. (Agricultural Heritage Museum photo)

Hall) and the Student Union, later to be named after him. The Student Association had to be incorporated in order to qualify for the program.

Unfortunately, as the building program progressed, Dr. Pugsley's health became precarious. One of my great tests occurred when I was called to his home and found him reclining on a couch in his study. He asked me to pick out the furniture for the new Union and the two dormitories. He explained that there were definite limitations as to designs and fabrics, but I was to select what I felt was the best. I swallowed hard and weakly asked: "May I have the help of Dr. Emily Davis, the Head of the Art Department?" He agreed, and Emily and I spent a day and a large part of the night making our selections. I was praying inwardly that the faculty, the students and the alumni would approve our choices. Fortunately, I heard no complaints when the Union opened on April 4, 1940. It had cost $200,000, and Duane Lake was the first manager.

The National Youth Administration, begun in June 1935, paid small stipends to over 400,000 youths nationwide in schools, colleges and graduate schools in compensation for work done after hours. This youth relief program not only counteracted the corroding effects of enforced idleness, but also equipped the rising generation more adequately for their

Construction starts on Pugsley Union in 1939. (1940 Jack Rabbit photo)

New Pugsley Union opened on April 4, 1940. It immediately became State's grand central station and the students' social center. (1940 Jack Rabbit photo)

life work and, by the same token, delayed their entrance into the already overcrowded labor market.

State profited from this influx of N.Y.A. assistance, because our budgets were so lean, and secretarial help had been reduced to a minimum. Since I always had late afternoon committee meetings, my N.Y.A. help was left alone in my office. I worried a little about the quality of English used by them in telephone calls, and most of them did not have any history background. The result was a horrendous confusion when they filed *New York Times* clippings for my history folders. During the thirties and early forties the *New York Times* had a photo section, which contained invaluable materials—but only if filed properly. I must confess that I still had some of those history files to destroy after I retired and left my last office in Scobey Hall.

FRIENDS, JOYS AND SADNESS

MEMORABLE FRIENDS

Life was not all excitement, dances and tea parties, but it seemed that much of my time was spent on such endeavors.

1941 students dancing the stocking foot conga kick in the Bunny Ballroom. (1942 Jack Rabbit photo)

One of my primary roles was to present about a third of the lectures to freshmen on orientation to college. In those early days, these lectures, for both men and women, were held in the auditorium. (Later, I delivered them separately to students in the different colleges, with my last freshman lecture on human engineering in 1971 to the engineers.) The lectures covered topics such as dating, dancing, table manners, restaurant dining, introductions, teas, receptions, balls and weddings. Occasionally

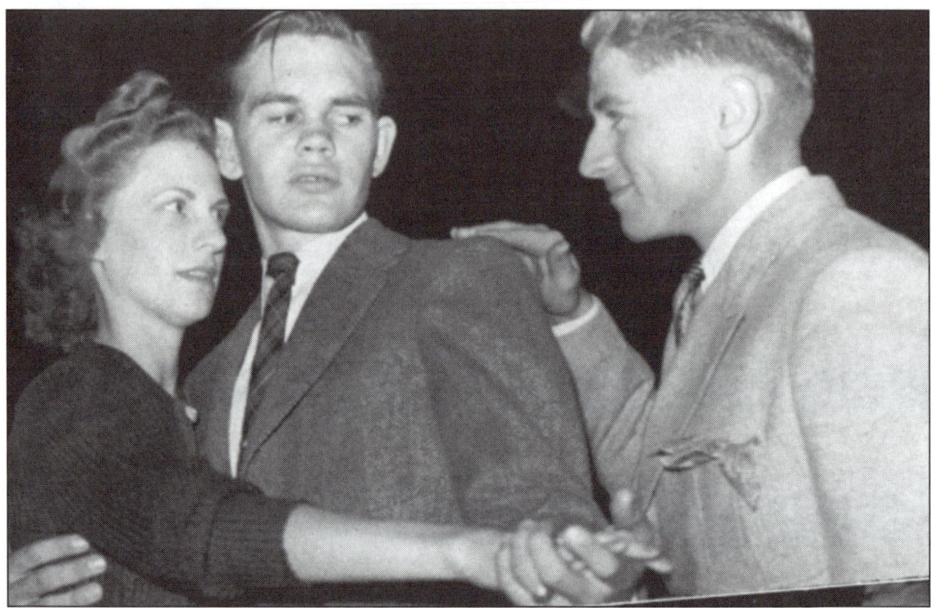

Wally Johnson and Evelyn Schultz following Dean Volstorff's advice here as they experience a "cut in" by an unidentified freshman at the 1941 Freshman Mixer. (1942 Jack Rabbit photo)

a faculty person would assist me in demonstrations. As I've mentioned, Dr. Ward Miller always helped to demonstrate correct dancing positions. We showed how awful arm pumping looked, or what cuddling did to bodylines, or how playing a saxophone down the spine of a girl really looked and felt. I always reminded the women that the left hand should be light as a feather on her partner's right shoulder. Our exaggerations helped students to remember.

One young man, later a Regent, told me that as he was coming into Guadalcanal during World War II, he stood alone with his private thoughts on the deck of a ship about to land. At that moment, he vowed that if he lived through the war he would return to State for the Military Ball in his dress uniform, to dance with the Dean of Women, and do all the things you were not supposed to do on the dance floor. After the war, he did return in full dress and came up with some surprising dance floor innovations of his own! The Dean of Pharmacy sent a student out on the dance floor to rescue me, believing that my partner was intoxicated. We both were intoxicated, of course, but with laughter!

Learning correct dancing positions was not very helpful, if students did not know how to dance. Many new students had never had any instruction in ballroom dancing, and some of their parents were opposed to dancing. Perhaps there was good reason for parental concern, because many of the small town dances were not the most wholesome affairs from the tales I heard from students. At any rate, I arranged for ballroom dancing classes in the sunroom, acting as instructor until I could persuade some capable senior women to accept the challenge, which they did without remuneration. As dances at State were frequent, I decided to ask the Board of Control to sponsor the lessons and pay a student instructor. To avoid embarrassment, separate classes for men and women were held until the basic skills were acquired, and then the classes were combined. After the Pugsley Union opened in the spring of 1940 and their program became operational, the Union Board sponsored the dancing classes, which were continued for many years.

Mary Nelson, sponsored by the Board of Control, helps students learn what they are supposed to do on the dance floor. (1952 Jack Rabbit photo)

One afternoon, Ken Anderson, editor of the *Collegian*, came to my office in Wecota Hall and insisted that I ride out of town with him so that we could discuss a problem. I was somewhat reluctant because his automobile was reputed to have bad brakes, but he was so serious, I decided to take the risk. When we were several miles out of town, he pulled off on a dirt side road.

"What is the problem?" I asked. After several attempts at explanation, he finally admitted that he wanted me to teach him to dance right then and there because he was too embarrassed to take the dancing classes.

"I've never even taken a date to a dance," he said sheepishly. The dirt road wasn't exactly a ballroom floor, but I did give him some basic instruction and later persuaded a sympathetic senior girl to accept a date with him for his maiden adventure on the dance floor. Ken was a popular student on campus, but that night he mystified all of his dance partners, except his date, by paying absolutely no attention to them, instead muttering to himself words like, "Side step-step, one-two-three step." To this day Ken thinks that his very happy marriage was due partially to the fact that I helped him to learn to dance.

Dr. N.E. Hansen, credited with gradually introducing dancing at faculty parties, was still attending formal dances in formal attire when I arrived on campus. His shows of chrysanthemum were a marvel of beauty, and his scientific work greatly benefitted the state of South Dakota. Whenever I gave a talk on international affairs, I could count on seeing Dr. Hansen in the audience, especially if the topic had anything to do with Russia.

In addition to dances, we had summer school picnics, often held at Lake Campbell, where the faculty joined the students on the roller skating rink. Dr. Ward Miller was most dexterous and talented in this skill. I felt very comfortable skating with him, although I felt somewhat guilty of interrupting his solo performances.

Hay rides, sleigh rides, and treasure hunts were frequent student and faculty activities as well. They were fun and not expensive. On one of my first faculty treasure hunts, one of the clues for my partner and me was "The flying trapeze on the Dean's hen coop." Although the other clues had been rather simple to decipher, this one was a puzzle. Eventually, I was certain that it had something to do with the fire escape stairs on the outside of Wecota Hall in the President's garden.

As my partner and I were hunting this area for a clue, a maintenance man suddenly appeared from the shrubbery, challenging us. He was startled and most apologetic when he discovered the Dean of Women and an English professor, and not someone attempting to break into the hall. We

Dr. N.E. Hansen, known for bringing new horticulture plants and legume crops to South Dakota from Russia, is also credited with introducing dancing at faculty parties. (Agricultural Heritage Museum photo)

hastily explained our presence and what we were seeking, but he was unable to help us

Later we learned that instead of dallying about the President's garden, we were supposed to have sung "The Daring Young Man on the Flying Trapeze" in the Wecota Hall lobby in order to obtain the next clue from my assistant, Mrs. Gertrude McKnight. She relished that story of our apprehension and repeated it often.

Before World War II, there was an active Little Theater group, which I thoroughly enjoyed. Casey Jarchow, popular History professor, was usually the male star. The dormitory residents were delighted when I took part. Their joy mostly stemmed from my absence from Wecota and the hope that they might keep their dates out later, as Mrs. McKnight had to check on Wenona Hall residents first, before doing my chores.

In my first role, I had to play the part of an Irish washerwoman who slurped her soup on stage and did an Irish jig. The stage of the former high school auditorium was quite small, and we were very close to the audience. On opening night, I discovered that my dormitory students and their dates occupied most of the front row seats. Despite their limited resources, they had saved their money for this occasion.

Because of those limited resources, many young women made their own clothing. More often than not, at the various meetings of women's groups I attended, the handiwork seemed more important than the programming. I will admit that I would rather have seen their eyes when I spoke to them instead of watching them counting stitches. However, in order to conform, I purchased some white rayon yarn and chose an Irish picot stitch with the intention of crocheting a dinner blouse. For months and months I carried the project with me to meetings, including our little theater group. Finally, one of the members of the English Department offered to give me a dinner party for the debut of the blouse as an incentive for me to complete the project. While listening intently to the radio, following the details of King Edward VIII and Wallis Warfield Simpson and the abdication crisis, I finally finished the blouse. If I do say so myself, it was lovely, long sleeves that pointed at the wrist, a cowl neckline in front and a modest V in back. Since it was time for the Women's Self Government association's formal tea for the faculty, I decided to surprise my doubting friends and wear the finished product.

I was thoroughly enjoying the faculty tea, when Dr. George Smock, head of the English Department, and his wife came through the receiving line almost at the end.

"I see that you are wearing the dinner blouse, but you did not finish it?" he said.

Puzzled, I reached back, and the "modest" V was down below my waist. To my horror, I also realized that the sleeves had been elongating as I had unconsciously pushed them up again and again at the wrists, producing a series of rumpled folds to my elbows. The short peplum blouse had become decidedly tunic in length. I had no one to blame but myself. The combination of rayon yarn and picot stitch had caused the blouse to elongate indefinitely. No amount of subsequent blocking attempts could rescue it. It looked as though it had been designed for an orangutan!

Years later, the blouse saw its only other public appearance. Frank Schultz, Dean of General Science,

Frank Schultz, Dean of General Science from 1942 to 1955 and Dean of Science and Applied Arts from 1955 to 1972. (Instructional Technologies Center photo)

called me to ask if I had any formal that he might possibly wear to dress as a woman for a Kiwanis party. I offered the blouse, knowing it would stretch to fit anyone, if he could find a long skirt. As he was not on campus when the blouse made its first appearance, he did not know the hazards involved in wearing this original creation. His wife was out of town the night of the Kiwanis program, and he called me, embarrassed, to ask which way was the front of the blouse. I promptly advised him to reverse the blouse, because the neglotage belonged in the back. I had a hilarious vision of the deep V and the dean's chest.

I think, however, that I made more appearances on campus in absurd outfits than any other faculty member. Often times, I subjected myself to ridicule for the benefit of the students. I loved attending student assemblies. The students themselves made assemblies sheer fun. They would bring in little German bands to play for candidates at Students' Association election time to give a little zeal to the campaigns. Other times, they planned philanthropic events, enlisting the help of faculty supporters.

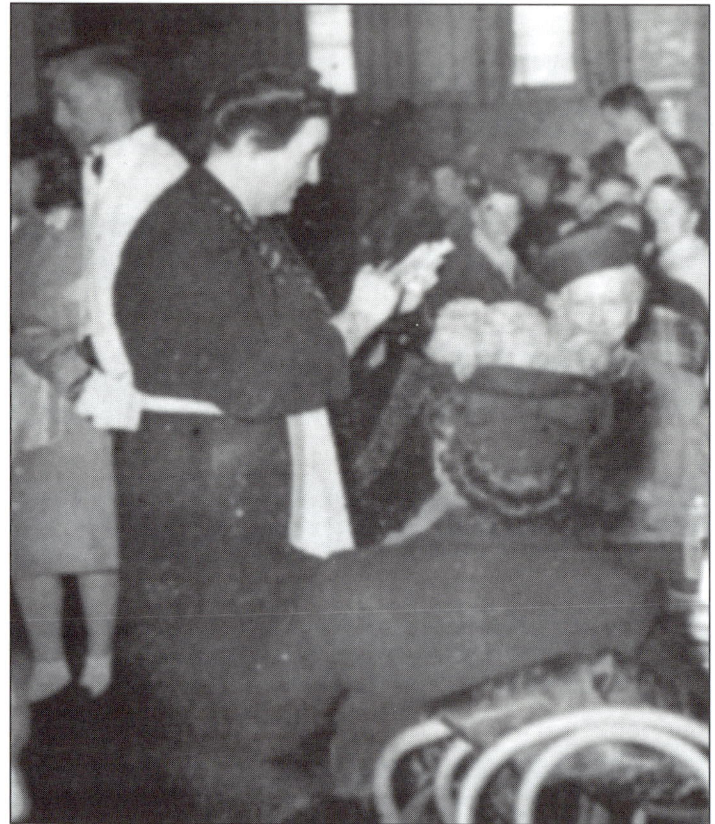

For eighteen dollars, two brothers from Watertown purchased Dean Volstorff's services in a charity auction to serve meals in the Old Jungle of the Pugsley Union from noon to 2 p.m. (1948 Jack Rabbit photo)

For one worthy cause, I agreed to participate in an auction of faculty services. For eighteen dollars, two brothers from Watertown purchased my services to serve meals in the Old Jungle of the Pugsley Union from noon to 2 p.m.—that very day!

As student assemblies were held at 11 a.m. with morning class periods shortened, I had to hurry to the Jungle to live up to my end of the bargain. Once there, I received a white jacket that was very ill-fitting and made me look ridiculous. Nevertheless, I started taking orders. Of course, I did not know the numbers of my assigned booths and tables, or the complete possibilities of the menu. It was Farm and Home week, and the farm women of the area were startled to see me taking orders, since I had been a guest speaker on their program earlier in the week. None of them wanted the special of the day! I also had a booth of young men from India and another of Latin American students, none of whom apparently had been at the assembly, and they attempted to rise each time I came to their booth.

Thankfully, one helpful engineering student made a chart of my booths and tables and explained the menu and ordering procedure. I lived through the ordeal and got my tabletops cleaned by 2 p.m., while a few faculty members and the brothers who had purchased my services looked on. There they sat; grinning like a pair of Cheshire cats; loitering over their food and watching me perform as an inexperienced waitress. Those two lads had plenty of money and usually had their lunches at the local hotel. They could afford to be ostentatious at my expense.

The social calendar in the early thirties included more formal affairs: the Military Ball, Junior-Senior Prom, Ag Dinner Dance, Officer's Mess Dinner Dance, and the Engineer's Dinner Dance, plus informal dances every week. To repay the hospitality of the men on campus, women organized the Coed Ball in the spring of 1933, a tradition that continued until 1981.

Receiving line at the 1952 Coed Ball. Dean Volstorff started the Coed Ball in 1933 and it continued until 1981. (1953 Jack Rabbit photo)

The early Coed Ball was a formal dinner dance. The dances were held in the basement cafeteria of Wecota Hall. Each year a new theme was used for decorations, sometimes affecting the menu. The women invited the men of their choice, arranged the dance program and provided a boutonniere, usually a carnation, for their escorts. The date's only expense was a corsage. Some unusual couples frequently appeared. The young men were so flattered to be invited that they sometimes accepted an invitation while forgetting that another girlfriend might have first priority. In 1940, the ball was moved to the Bunny Ballroom in the new Pugsley Student Union. The dinner was omitted and more efforts went into decorations and favors.

In addition to repaying the men for all the social events the women were escorted to, the experience of putting on the ball was good for the women. In the years I served as adviser, the ball never lost money and was enthusiastically supported by the women students. Upon completion of the new wing to the Pugsley Union, the Coed Ball was moved to the Christy Ballroom and finally to the Volstorff Ballroom.

The ball was scheduled in the spring to avoid late winter storms, which plagued us on several occasions when the orchestras arrived late or got snowbound. Spring dates created a more romantic mood, and many engagement rings would appear the day of the ball or shortly thereafter.

Interest in the dance died somewhat after 1973 because the Association of Women Students, which sponsored the ball, suffered from a lack of participation and disbanded. For several years, other organizations placed bids to sponsor the dance. The Greek system of social fraternities and sororities were awarded the dance on a permanent basis. They decided, however, not to sponsor a ball in 1982, and thus this tradition, like so many others, died. Gone too from the State calendar today are the formal balls and weekly dances where students dressed up for the dance with faculty chaperones present.

Instead there is bar-hopping for the majority of our students, as the important mid-week and weekend activities. Here students find a totally different atmosphere, with too much drinking, very casual dress, late hours and driving hazards. It's an expensive social life, too, although my information is not first-hand. This is despite rumors to the contrary, sparked by the red Mercury I owned. A student had one like it, and his was parked frequently at the Lucky Lady and similar places, which created a little confusion and embarrassment for me. Though students knew better, they could not resist teasing me about my car being seen parked at various bars.

All-college assemblies finally fell victim to greatly increased enrollments, the lack of space in the auditorium, and complicated scheduling

David Pearson was Students' Association President in 1939 when the plans for the 1940 Pugsley Student Union were made. (1939 Jack Rabbit photo)

David F. Pearson served under President Briggs and Berg from 1957 to 1980 as Assistant Professor, Assistant to the President, Director of Development and Vice President for Administration. He was a key administrator in the planning and construction of the 1973 Student Union. (1967 Jack Rabbit photo)

of classes. When the Students' Association felt the need for a mass meeting, they held it in the Old Barn. Somehow over the years, the enthusiasm for student activities declined from the days when David Pearson was Student President and would plead for the students to get that old feeling during Hobo Week.

Socializing in the residence halls has changed a great deal over the years, too. I remember February of 1936, when I was marooned for two solid weeks in the women's dormitories because of an energy crisis. We had unseasonably low temperatures and blizzards every week from January 20 for two whole months. On February 10, classes were suspended to save the ebbing fuel supply because the trains were not able to get through the high drifts. Very limited budgets prevented acquiring adequate stockpiles earlier in the season.

During the break from classes, the women's dormitories allowed male visitors from 9 a.m. to 10:30 p.m. I felt as though I was running a nightclub. There was dancing all day in the sunroom, and the tiny tea room in Wenona Hall was constantly in use as students made popcorn, fudge and taffy. By the time classes resumed, everyone was saturated with sweets and dancing, and we all welcomed a normal schedule of classes.

My apartment had been inhabited by student guests much of the time, reading my *New York Times*, and my books of poetry. Most students had never heard of Kahlil Gibran, Rabindranath Cagore, Lew Sarett, or even Elizabeth Barrett Browning. Don Mall, a Brookings lad, wrote a long, hilarious letter, describing my life during this hectic period and sent it to my mother. Don was later killed in the effort to re-invade Burma during World War II. His last letter to me was a very diverting one, describing how they were bivouacked on the roof of a maharaja's palace and his experience in India.

Students who lived nearby went home during the energy crisis, but most students stayed with friends on campus to prevent being stranded. The men's and women's dormitories were heated, but only sufficient heat to prevent freeze-up was allowed in all the other campus buildings. The temperatures were bone chilling. February 10, 1936, it was 30 degrees below zero, on Valentine's Day. And on a farm six miles east of Brookings the thermometer registered 40 degrees below zero on February 15. Classes were not resumed until February 24. Many faculty members ate in the Wecota Cafeteria because it was warmer than their homes.

In June of 1936, it was already heating up for the summer. In the interval between the close of the regular college year and the summer session, I was invited to go to the Black Hills with Captain Pembroke E. Browner, Head of the Department of Military Science and Tactics, his wife Mabel, and their eight-year-old son, Pem. I knew I would enjoy the trip and the company of young Pem, who for some reason was thoroughly devoted to me. The Browner family lived where Pugsley Hall is now located, and Pem would visit me frequently in Wecota Hall—visits which were refreshing for me but concerned his parents because of my hectic schedule.

There were no car air conditioners, and when we arrived in Pierre for lunch, we sought relief in a drug store with ceiling fans. As we sat in a small booth, Mabel began warning Pem about the possibility of encountering dangerous bears in the Black Hills.

As Mabel continued her warning, I saw a large dark brown Labrador retriever enter the drug store with a young man. Mabel, caught up in her lecture, didn't see the dog until its head was in her lap, whereupon she shrieked, "It's a bear!" Her shrill Texas voice alerted everyone to our presence. I heard Pem say with some slight disgust: "M-O-T-H-E-R, it is only a dog."

When we finally reached Deadwood, there was a carnival taking place, and rooms were scarce. I ended up in one with only a skylight. A tropical bird in the lobby made disturbing, raucous noises all night, and with the carnival goers causing a ruckus, I never lost consciousness in that hot, stuffy room. Some of the nocturnal conversations were not exactly fitting for a Dean of Women to hear. I got up once after a knock on my door and placed two chairs in front of it, just in case.

The next morning at breakfast, Pem announced that we were going to climb Mt. Rushmore all the way to the top of Washington's head.

Mount Rushmore in the Black Hills, under construction. (Agricultural Heritage Museum photo)

Fortunately, I was much younger then, and several cups of coffee cleared my groggy head. At Mt. Rushmore, wooden planks allowed visitors to gradually climb the mountainside. When we were about three-fourths of the way up, and my legs were wobbling; a siren went off, warning us to seek shelter on the top of Washington's head. The workmen were about to blast off a piece of Jefferson's cravat. Of course, the last lap was straight up a ladder. Pem made it easily, along with his mother. Captain Browner was behind me, I think because he noticed my sheer fright and very uncertain legs. With his encouragement and Pem's, I made it to the top. Once the blast dust had settled, we surveyed the view from our precarious perch on Washington's aristocratic forehead behind only a single wooden rail to protect us from sliding off the nose. The view was magnificent, but I felt as though I would be sailing off to eternity if I looked down. The trip down Mt. Rushmore was comparatively uneventful, except for my nervousness and inability to walk in a straight line. Perhaps it was tourists like me who convinced park officials to discontinue public climbing of Mt. Rushmore shortly after our visit.

We explored every cave in the hills. Some were quite primitive, and I suffered claustrophobia in every one. We climbed, bent, stooped, and crawled through them. Captain Browner remarked that he was certainly getting into physical shape for summer camp, but I questioned whether I would survive. Once a guide boosted me up by giving my posterior support. Thereafter, I moved with extreme caution, prodded on by sheer embarrassment. Unfortunately, we did not explore the civilized Wind Cave. Pem must not have known about it.

Captain Browner was later on General MacArthur's staff in the Asiatic Theater in World War II, as well as Captain Robert Vesey, who was also stationed at State at the same time. Captain Vesey was killed on the Bataan death march, and Captain Browner survived the war. The friendship and hospitality of the Browners meant a great deal to me in those early years, when I was making the personal adjustment to being a Dean of Women—poles apart from my former student days in Evanston.

I wasn't an easy friend to have. I recall one occasion when Mrs. Browner and I were planning a bridge party at her home. I had suggested that we freeze some ginger ale ice cubes to be used in a fresh fruit cup. Unfortunately, I filled the trays too full and we could not dislodge them from the freezer unit. Captain Browner had to come home and rescue the cubes. My gourmet instincts were sound, but knowledge of physics was not.

Another time, when I was very ill with the flu and a sinus infection, Mabel Browner brought over a thermos of hot lemonade that put me under a deep sleep for twelve hours. Before it took effect, however, she saved a girl's possessions in a dormitory room, after a hair dryer caught the room draperies on fire, by dousing the flame with a wastebasket of water. Later, she confessed that she worried that I might awaken in the night and start singing something ridiculous.

Captain Vesey's wife, Toots, was a gourmet cook who entertained beautifully—curry and oriental dishes, as well as pheasants stuffed with wild rice. Toots was an authority on antique glass and oriental porcelains and ceramics, as well as a delightful, animate person. Her two young daughters were equally interesting. Captain Vesey gave me a nickname, the Chinese equivalent of the highest in culture, which I never learned to pronounce. At a Military Ball he would say: "This is my dance with (and give the Chinese phrase)", or say, "Make way!" and repeat the nickname. Nobody but Robert and Toots knew what it meant.

I enjoyed hearing about their army life. Captain Vesey was barely out of West Point. He graduated early because of World War I. He was assigned to help supervise the unloading of American supplies on the wharves in France, an incredible experience for him among the French dockhands. Both the Veseys and the Browners told of experiences in Borneo, China and the Philippines, as well as the merits and demerits of their commanding officers.

During the '30s, The Veseys, an English professor and I took a course in Italian. Miss Catherine MacLaggan taught foreign languages. She offered the Italian course for a few talented vocal music students. We availed ourselves of the opportunity. As a French minor, I had difficulty using a broader pronunciation of Italian, having a tendency to clip the words short, like French terms.

Miss MacLaggan insisted that we participate fully, even though we were just auditing the class. We had to memorize a number of poems. One of our assignments was to learn the celebrated *Miserere* from the opera *Il Trovatore* in Italian. It is one of the more beautiful numbers in the entire realm of music. I was saying it to myself one evening when I was turning on the lights in Wecota Lounge. A student and her date asked what I was saying. They explained that they had just heard a student singing the same song, at the top of his lungs, as he came down the library steps. I explained that it was the *Miserere* chant from *Il Trovatore* and that the student was probably from our Italian class.

Later that week, the Veseys and I were attending a basketball game together and we practiced the *Miserere*. The *Collegian* reported later that the Dean of Women and Captain and Mrs. Vesey were praying for the basketball players!

After World War II and her husband's death, Mrs. Vesey took a boat trip to the Philippines to visit her married daughter, whose husband was stationed there. On board she met a member of the State Department, assigned to the Far Eastern section, and he fell in love with her. They were married later, and he served as ambassador to Japan and later to Indonesia. They retired to Honolulu, where she died.

There were other memorable couples, too. I remember Rollins "Dick" Emmerich, a football player and an outstanding military student. When he

Richard 'Dick' Emmerich '36 was Cadet Colonel while a student. In 1943-44 he returned to State as commander of the Army Specialized Training Unit. (1942 Jack Rabbit photo)

was a senior, he haunted the History office for a week, vainly trying to catch me at my class time. Finally, Casey Jarchow, professor of History, asked Dick what he wanted. Well, he had to talk to Dean Volstorff and it was personal and very important. Casey gave him my class schedule and then suggested that he go to see me in the Women's Dormitories. But Dick was bashful and did not want to seek me out in the dormitory, so he waited for me after my class. What was the problem? He had been elected Cadet Colonel and he had to go to the Military Ball, but he had not been dating any girls. He did not know a single girl that he dared ask for fear she would refuse.

I laughed and said, "Dick, there are dozens of girls who would be thrilled to go to the Military Ball with the Cadet Colonel and a handsome football hero. And, I have an easy solution for you. Do you know who will be elected Honorary Cadet Colonel? She will obviously have to go the ball, too, and even if she is practically engaged to someone, she could still go with you in your mutual, official capacities."

He said she would be elected in a couple of days and smiled with relief that there was a solution to his personal problem. He asked her practically the moment she was selected.

The night of that Military Ball the stardust fell on Dick and on Helen Frothinger. They were holding hands, beaming and radiant. It was true love from that moment in their lives. They both told me that they had had a very wonderful evening. Thus, was started the Emmerich dynasty, which I have enjoyed watching over the years. At least three of their girls attended State, and all of their children have been outstanding. Dick and his brother Jim were among the most avid supporters of State.

Colonel Rollin S. Emmerich, who graduated in 1936, returned to South Dakota State College in 1940 and served in the department of Military Science and Tactics until 1943 when the program was interrupted by the war. In 1943-44 he commanded the Army Specialized Training Unit stationed at State. He served with the Korean Military Advisory Group and was attached to the Third ROK Division, the first unit of the UN forces to cross the 38th Parallel on the drive northward. He helped evacuate the families of American personnel at his headquarters, placed himself in command of the disorganized and confused KMAG Headquarters in Pusan and organized American troops, supplies, and facilities as they began pouring into Korea. He retired to Denver with Helen, where he enjoyed fishing, hunting in Canada, wood carving and his grandchildren.

Jim Emmerich, former South Dakota State University track coach, is a member of five halls of fame. He was a college division All-American football player and top student at State. He coached two cross-country and one track national championship, plus ten North Central Conference (NCC) track titles from 1947 to 1960. His Jackrabbit cross-country teams never lost to another NCC opponent. Jim also worked as a trainer for United States teams at three summer Olympics. He was the head trainer of the United States 1964 summer Olympic team in Tokyo and was a U.S. trainer during the Melbourne Games in 1956. He worked with America's Mexico City team in 1968 and with the Winter Olympic hockey team in 1964. He was the head U.S. trainer during the 1959 Pan American Games in Chicago.

Starting as an all-American football player and a top student at State, Jim Emmerich coached track and field at SDSU from October 1940 to September 1960 with a four-year war leave in the '40s. He was a legend in North Central Conference coaching history. (Instructional Technologies Center photo)

In 1975 Jim started a unique "dollar a day" scholarship program at State, which has grown to provide assistance to athletes in five areas. He gave so much of himself to our youth and to our state. He had the extraordinary ability as a trainer to demand superior performances. Jim, a legend in North Central Conference history, passed away in 1993.

Another friend of mine from those early days was Raymond "Red" Cully. During the depression students worked every spare minute to earn enough money to remain in college. Wages were only fifteen to twenty-five cents an hour, depending on the skills required. Red painted signs for the Jenny Gray apparel store (window signs were cheaper than advertising space in the paper), and played the piano in a student dance orchestra. He was very artistic and talented, and shortly before his graduation, his uncle offered to help finance graduate study in art in Washington, D.C. I remember counseling him to accept, because if he had the training, he could easily repay his uncle at a later date. He was very reluctant to incur an obligation in those depression days, but he finally accepted the offer. Years later he was the art director of a prominent Washington newspaper and President Leinbach suggested his name to the Head of Printing and Journalism Department as a speaker for Newspaper Editors Day at State.

A few years later, right in the middle of a serious Administrative Council meeting, President Leinbach suddenly looked at me and said: "I met one of your former boyfriends in Washington at the Alumni meeting, and he is coming here for Newspaper Day." I was somewhat embarrassed, but happy to know that Red had made a name for himself. I had not seen him since his graduation.

I was assigned to take Red to the banquet. As usual my schedule got hectic at the office, and I called him and said that I would be a little late, because I still had to change attire. To which he replied: "I will get a taxi and help you!" I laughed and explained that I meant my clothing, not the tire on my car. "I do not need a gentleman-in-waiting yet," I said.

Finally, I met him and drove to the banquet, happily noting his beautiful cashmere coat and off-white pigskin gloves—such a vivid contrast to his lean student days. But to this day I have never again used the expression change attire. I change my clothes or dress for dinner!

I first met Red at an open house where he was playing for a dance in the sunroom. I had visited informally with the orchestra members and later he actually apologized for anything he might have said to me, because he had not known he was talking to the Dean of Women. Later that year, he escorted me to a Coed Ball, held in Wecota Cafeteria, and I inadvertently missed a scheduled dance with an Education professor, whose wife was quite upset, because she really wanted to dance with Red. I missed the appointment because I was distracted by the breaking of the base for my antique cut-glass punch bowl. When the punch had been used up, two of the cafeteria helpers had pulled two tables apart and almost broke both the bowl as well as the base. The cut-glass punch bowl and ladle were an early purchase of mine, and I was really upset when the base was broken, leaving the bowl with a very small round base that would not balance it. Years later, a young lieutenant in the Air Force made a myrtle wood base for the punch bowl, which we then used in our dining room. I still think that Red was one of the best dancing partners I ever had at State. We mollified the Education professor and his wife by giving them the last dance at the Coed Ball.

Living in the dormitories those early years, before we were forced to vacate the halls for the army units during World War II, I shared in all kinds of successes in the students' lives: the excitement of obtaining a summer job, a first permanent position, a new formal or a diamond engagement ring (which I occasionally saw even before the intended recipient did), the exciting new date who was Mr. Right and all the joyful, happy times in a coed's life.

TIMES OF SADNESS

There were sad times as well. I was visiting with a female senior student in my office early in my career at State when the telephone rang. It was Dr. Myron Tank.

"Dean Volstorff," he said, "Please come to the hospital. Dorothy Dokin has been killed."

I was so shocked that I could not even replace the phone on the cradle, and the student in my office stared at me in consternation. I finally regained my composure sufficiently to explain what had happened and left in a hurry.

At the hospital one member of the group in the car accident was in surgery, and Dorothy's date was incoherent, wandering about bloody and battered. I knew immediately that I wasn't prepared for this first emergency. I recalled the night before, when Dorothy came into my office to show me her new flowered formal that she was wearing to the dinner dance. Just a few short hours ago, after the dance, she had brought in all the favors she had received to show me. She was radiant with happiness that night, and I was anguished by her death.

"She said that she wanted to go to Sioux Falls tomorrow to play golf, and we checked her parental approval list on file," I approved the out of town trip.

Dr. Tank took one look at me and said, "Please sit down. We don't need a fainting problem just now."

After a few moments of collecting myself, I took comfort in following through with emergency procedures. It was difficult talking to the sheriff involved and even more so contacting her parents, who were understandably overwhelmed with grief, but it became easier for me to deal with the situation by providing help to others.

The years were to bring more of these tragic moments. I never grew accustomed to identifying accident victims, nor sharing with a young woman the ghastly news of the wartime death of a sweetheart, brother or father. But that first emergency is still etched in my mind as clearly as though it happened yesterday.

It seems that much has changed since my early days at State. There used to be Memorial Day assemblies, first in the auditorium and then in Liberty Grove, where a fresh wreath was placed on the stone each spring.

Memorial Day program in Liberty Grove, north of the Lincoln Library. (1946 Jack Rabbit photo)

We would stand quietly for an honor salute by the crack rifle squad, after the lists of names were read of those who gave their lives during the First World War. After World War II, these services were very painful for me, as memories surged when the names of the young men were read— all one hundred and eleven. The Korean War added eight more names, and eleven more were sacrificed in the difficult Vietnam conflict.

I also recall vividly the first time that I learned that Brookings fire-fighters were volunteers. A few weeks after my arrival in Brookings, I was ordering supplies for a tea at the Service Grocery, which specialized in home deliveries and special courtesies to its patrons. Cash Wells, the clerk who was taking my order, suddenly threw off his white apron and hurtled out of the store, racing to the fire station so that he could be the first one there for the privilege of driving the truck. Coming from a large city where emergency noises were a part of daily life, I had not even heard the fire alarm.

One Sunday morning I was awakened at 3 a.m. by choking smoke, and I groped my way to the telephone to call the fire department. Then, covering my mouth with a cloth, I sought the source of the fire.

Smoke was billowing out of the transom of the tearoom, next to the sunroom. A huge coffeepot with a mixture of eggs and coffee had boiled down to cinders. I turned off the electric plate and opened the windows of the sun-room, just in time to greet the fire fighters and President Pugsley, whose home was next to Wecota Hall.

Groups of sleepy coeds were congregating outside of both dormitories. I spent the next hour greeting college staff and male students, explaining that it was just coffee grounds that caused the smoke and fire alarm.

Earlier in the evening, a play had been presented for a club meeting in the sunroom, and my assistant, Mrs. McKnight, had been one of the hostesses. Good coffee in those days was always made with eggs—a mixture bound to surpass any concocted lab odor in its potency when burned to a crisp! I vowed then and there to always check the tearoom as part of my nightly routine after locking the entrance doors.

THE WINDS OF WAR

As the decade of the nineteen thirties drew to a close, events in Europe cast their shadows on the rest of the world. The last week of August 1939, I sprained my right ankle by a fall on concrete steps at my home in Elgin, Illinois—a very serious inconvenience when I drove back to Brookings using my left foot on the accelerator. My real anguish and worry, however, was the war in Europe. Despite President Roosevelt's stated position that the country could stay out of the war in Europe, it was evident that conflict was on its way, and I would be 600 miles away from my family. I arrived in Brookings mid-day on Friday, September 1, in time to be greeted by three headlines across the top of page one in the *Argus Leader*:

"Nazis Invade Poland, Bomb Warsaw"

"Poles Ask Aid from England and France"

"President Says America Can Keep Out of War"

Hitler changed the world that day. This was despite the fact that the war in Europe after his conquest of Poland seemed to become a "phony" war, or "Sietz Krig" as some journalists termed it. There was inactivity between opposing forces on France's Maginot line and German's Siegfried line. Only the air forces were in some action, and German submarines roamed the high seas.

Then in April 1940, Hitler invaded Denmark and Norway. In May, he sent his army and air force against the Netherlands, Belgium and Luxembourg. Hitler's tanks went around the Maginot line and drove the combined British and French off the continent at Dunkirk.

We saw South Dakota, like the nation, approach recovery from the depression just before the war crisis heightened. Fortunately, the weather cycle had changed for the better, as the dust bowl finally ended.

A driving blizzard on November 11, 1940, canceled the ROTC parade plans and extended Armistice vacations an extra day. I had given a dinner party with the head of the Art Department at her home that night. Our guests were able to get to their homes, but I stayed overnight to help with clean-up operations. The next day I was completely marooned by impassable drifts. Mae Austin, then manager of the book-

Brookings County Press

"Brookings County's Newsiest Weekly Newspaper"

Sixty-First Year—Established Feb. 20, 1879   BROOKINGS COUNTY PRESS—BROOKINGS, S. D. NOVEMBER 14, 1940   NUMBER 36

MOST DESTRUCTIVE STORM IN FIFTY YEARS HITS BROOKINGS AREA MONDAY

• •

Armistice Day—1940—will go down in Brookings history as the most complete blockade this community has known before Christmas in the automobile age. Highways and railways were blocked, streets were blocked, telephone lines and telegraph lines were "out of order," and all public functions were cancelled, and there was nothing to do much except to listen to the radio and watch the wind whirl the snow in blinding clouds and pack it in huge drifts. Both city schools and college extended their Armistice Day observance to cover Tuesday, as the storm still raged most of the day Tuesday.

• •

The November 11, 1940 'Armistice Day' blizzard was one of the most severe winter storms on record for the Upper Midwest. (George Norby's Historic Newspaper Collection)

store, arranged for one of her student roomers to rescue me with a sleigh. I arrived at Wecota Hall safely, if in an undignified manner, much to the relief of my assistant, Mrs. McKnight, who had managed both Wenona and Wecota Halls during my absence. Students straggled in one or two days late with monstrous tales of hardship and high snowdrifts.

One of the students who experienced that Armistice blizzard, Sherwood Berg, later was to be plagued with an early blizzard in November of 1975, when he was to be installed as President of South Dakota State University. Installation services were postponed several times and finally incorporated with fall commencement ceremonies.

The Military Ball was held on December 5, 1941, and Colonel Murphy beamed as the old armory filled to overflowing. Advanced ROTC members sighed with relief after selling enough tickets to pay for the band, "Red Nichols and His Five Pennies."

The Grand March at the December 5, 1941 Military Ball. (1942 Jack Rabbit photo)

The December 5, 1941 Military Ball with "Red Nichols and his Five Pennies" was the last big entertainment event before the war. (1942 Jack Rabbit photo)

PEARL HARBOR

The following Sunday I was listening to records of Christmas carols and making stenciled Christmas cards when the telephone in the Art Department rang, and my mood was rudely shattered by news of Japan's attack on Pearl Harbor. That night Professor Karl Theman's 180-member chorus sang of peace in the annual presentation of the "Messiah" to a packed auditorium of students, faculty and townspeople, everyone experiencing an alien emotion of fear and apprehension by the events of that Sunday morning.

The next day, December 8, 1941, students, faculty and townspeople assembled in the College Armory at 11 a.m. to hear President Roosevelt ask Congress for a declaration of war against Japan.

Two military airs were played by Christy's band, but the audience remained silent as the congressional applause for the President's speech roared through the speaker. The group in the Armory took a mass oath of allegiance and unanimously endorsed a letter by President Jackson and

December 8, 1941. Students, faculty and townspeople gather in the 'Barn' to listen to President Roosevelt as he asks congress to declare war on Japan. (1942 Jack Rabbit photo)

the student president, pledging the College's "complete support of the war effort." Students found it difficult to study in the next few days as the impact of the war grew even more critical with the U.S. declaration of war on Germany and Italy. Five days later, junior class President Robert Dailey, a navy man for four years before entering State in 1939, enlisted in the Navy Air Corps and withdrew from college. He was our first lad to join in the war effort. Later, he was to serve as a member of the Board of Regents in the post-war period. By registration time on January 5, 1942, quite a few faces were missing.

ADVERSITIES OF WAR

Keeping the college functioning during the war period was no small task for President Lyman E. Jackson, who arrived on campus in January 1941. Under his guidance, State maintained its personality and persevered despite many adversities and the urgent necessity of coordinating the college to meet both the army and civilian needs. Through it all, the President worked for a better college after the war.

War-enforced changes were common, as State students carried on amid a confusion of 7:30 a.m. classes, six-week terms, and 100-minute periods. Faculty and students alike found such a long stretch of straight intellectual labor fatiguing. Women had to endure rayon hose, which wrinkled around their legs like barber poles, and the Union served something called "margarine" in the Jungle. And worse yet, Hobo Day of 1942 was a casualty of the war, when Dr. Jackson dismissed college for two weeks so that students and faculty could harvest crops for the war effort. Some faculty as well as students had cuts and calluses on their hands from stacking corn into teepees. When

Lyman E. Jackson was President at State from 1940 to 1946. (Instructional Technologies Center photo)

Dean Volstorff rides her bicycle in the Hobo Day Parade during one of the war years. (Vivian Volstorff photo collection)

they returned, some alumni never forgave President Jackson for dismissing the Hobo Day tradition so summarily, even for the war. For the students it was the Hobo Day debacle, as half-built floats, whiskered faces and tattered clothes were thrown into discard. During the following years, the tradition was carried on in severely attenuated form.

Although rationing was necessary for the whole country to conserve fuel, rubber, and foodstuffs, President Roosevelt delayed imposing it until after the 1942 elections, almost a year after Pearl Harbor. In World War II, if you didn't have a war job or a medical degree or some other exemption, you got two gallons of gas a week. Bicycles were rationed, and you could buy only two pairs of shoes a year. Forget about needing new tires. Just about everything went to war—from mom's nylons to dad's garden hose. There were other shortages, too: tobacco, sugar, coffee, ice cream, meat, and most foodstuffs. Eventually, 40 percent of the country's vegetables were produced in backyard Victory Gardens.

Travel was impossible. Gas rationing began on the East Coast in 1942 because of tanker losses to German submarines. And yet no fewer than 200 Congressmen demanded and got "X" priorities, allowing themselves unlimited gasoline.

The biggest problem, though, was rubber. The Japanese seized the source of 90 percent of the world's rubber supply in the first three months of the war. Under the influence of the farm bloc, Congress adopted a plan to develop alcohol-based rubber, although it would be more expensive than the petroleum method. Finally, Roosevelt vetoed the congressional plan and moved ahead with the petroleum-based synthetic. By 1944 the United States produced 80 percent of the tons of rub-

Gene Burr, Chemistry professor and military advisor was an "unsung hero" during trying times. Prof. Burr worked long and hard with students to learn about service alternatives and help them prove they were worthy to stay in college. (1943 Jack Rabbit photo)

ber consumed by the war effort. Roosevelt also set the national speed limit at 35 miles per hour, while today's drivers scoff at 55.

World War II was the best thing to happen to hijackers since Prohibition, and the black market boomed. Counterfeiting ration stamps was such a prosperous operation that organized criminals took it over, much to the anger of patriotic Americans who resented their greed in such perilous times.

Probably the most pestered man on campus was Gene Burr, Chemistry Professor and one-man advisory board for troubled students. As military adviser, Burr compiled data on the numerous services and worked long and hard with students who proved they were worthy to stay in college. Gene Burr was one of the "unsung heroes" on campus during that trying time.

MILITARY TRAINEES

I shall never forget the arrival of the very first army unit one morning at about 5:30 a.m. at Wecota Cafeteria. Every window in Wecota and Wenona had girls looking out wondering what it would mean in their lives to have the army living in Wecota Annex. The army was elated to be served real eggs instead of dried ones for that first breakfast at State. My women residents gave the army some unscheduled fire drills, courtesy of a special button in the old bell room of Wecota. No one ever admitted to pushing it, but the sergeants and other members of the cadre took a very dim view of these unorthodox drills. Fortunately, I was not on the discipline committee in those days. I knew too much about campus shenanigans because I lived in the dormitories, and I was young at heart then.

The presence of military trainees using College facilities relieved the manpower shortage during these days of "Petticoat" rule. The armed forces personnel kept arriving and leaving at intervals between 1942 and 1945. Included were: Army Air Corps soldiers being trained in the Army Administration and Classification School; Air Corps Reserve men receiving preliminary instruction in ground work as pilots; Army Engineers; Army Specialized Training corps; and 17-year-old reservists.

The peak number of trainees on campus at any one time was 1,480. Dr. Jackson, in his report to the Regents in June 30, 1944, stated that 5,796 young people had gone through the programs, which were continued throughout 1945.

Armed forces personnel with duffel bags getting off the train in Brookings to use the SDSU campus for training. As many as 1480 trainees at one time kept arriving and leaving at intervals between 1942 and 1945. (1943 Jack Rabbit photo)

The effects of WW II were felt early in 1942 on our campus. Men were leaving for military service, and the class schedule was speeded up so students could finish classes before going into the service. ROTC was continued through the summer of 1942, so that cadets could graduate the following March and go on active duty. Then, the ROTC program at State was discontinued until after the war.

"FORTY-FOUR KINGS"

In March of 1943, 44 ROTC cadets from the Class of '44 who had been promised that they would be commissioned upon being taken into the service were ordered to report to Fort Snelling and then to Camp Wolters, Texas. When they arrived in Texas, their commissions were not delivered. They spent the summer in basic training as enlisted men learning heavy weapons. They protested, stating that they had signed contracts that would lead to commissions. Thus, they were returned to South Dakota State in September of 1943 until they could be issued orders to report for officer training. They formed a separate platoon under the ASTP (Army Student Training Program) then on campus. Due to their knowledge of the campus, group cohesiveness and the scarcity of male students on campus, they were dubbed "Forty-four Kings." This role did not last long. Three months later they were sent to Fort Benning for

Alumni Days 1997 reunion for the "Forty-four Kings". They were 44 ROTC cadets from the Class of '44 who formed a special military training platoon and left the campus in March of 1943 for Infantry Officers Candidate School at Fort Benning, GA. (State, the SDSU Alumni Association magazine photo)

Infantry Officers Candidate School. Sherwood O. Berg, later the president of State, was a member of this group. I doubt that any group of young men has ever brought as much distinction to their alma mater as that group of forty-four. All of them qualify as Distinguished Alumni.

I shall never forget the emotional picture of the "Forty-four Kings" departure en masse at the railroad station. Everyone was present. Sweethearts and sisters clung to their loved ones and tried desperately to restrain their emotions, emotions that later erupted into hysterics and tears at the dormitories. I had a very busy night trying to calm those young women, even though I myself had a great empathy with those girls that night, because I too was facing a personal emotional crisis. A beloved friend was dying of cancer, and his death was a watershed in my life.

I decided to stay with my State coeds to see them through the war. Then, I never left the campus.

"THE CHERUBS"

When the Army Engineering students occupied Wenona and Wecota Halls, the women had to move off campus to private homes. Four large homes were rented for freshman women. I took charge of one of the houses for two years and asked the students to identify their own leadership group because I was gone most of the time and needed a congenial, responsible team of leaders. Subsequently, the selected women called themselves "the cherubs."

My life was anything but dull while I was living in the Cherub House. One of the famous "cherub" families called themselves "The Available Eight." (Bernice E. Nelson/Buntley, Susan Smith/Schutz, Marian Schaeffer Christopherson, Marge Guindon Larson, Carol Danforth Williams, Marilyn Holmberg, Jeanne Perry Schiver, Betty Berry Tesar. They still communicate with each other.)

The cherubs nursed me through the abysmal Palm Sunday weekend when I lost my friend from cancer. Later they planned a lovely Mother's Day dinner for me, complete with a gardenia corsage—my favorite flower.

We shared joys and sorrows, were thrilled or saddened by the mails. I dreaded those late calls about casualties. Alas, some of the cherubs fell for lads who were shipped from here to England and then to a relatively quiet sector of France, or so the authorities thought, just in time to be hit with the Battle of the Bulge, without any battle experience at all. Fog prevented early retaliation. When the fog lifted, dead soldiers covered the attack area. That was not a pleasant sight for raw recruits. When we heard about the battle back home, there was some weeping and wailing until much later when sweethearts received mail from their loved ones. Some of those brief attachments later became permanent. The cherubs waited for our own lads to return.

Our telephone number in those days was almost the same as one of the local bootleggers, and we received some weird calls at our house, sometimes with a generous outpouring of profanity from an unhappy wife or customer before we could explain that they had called the wrong number.

The house had a masonite partition that separated my living room from that of the cherubs. One evening I was having a supper party for the Christys and Dean and Mrs. Schultz, when all of a sudden a loud and lusty version of "Old Man Mose" came from the other side of the masonite. My guests and I heard frantic steps on the stairs and then complete silence, as the songstress, Susan Smith, learned that I was giving a party. Thankfully, my startled guests took the surprise entertainment with good-natured amusement.

The cherub house was also a mouse motel. The pesky rodents were fond of fudge, dill pickles and potato chips. I had to be rescued numerous times, out of my unwillingness to set traps or release the victims. But my cherubs obligingly did these chores for me, knowing full well why we were infested. I had a complete trap line going all the time I lived there. When the cherubs were away on vacation, Emily Dans, head of the Art Department, would rescue me. Friends were wonderfully understanding of my one weakness.

MESSAGES OF TRAGEDY

Every coed wrote letters to servicemen: brothers, fathers, sweethearts, friends and classmates. Between classes they sought their own mail, read the war news and eventually received word of those receiving medals, some posthumously as the war progressed. I had the heartbreaking task of bringing many coeds the message of tragedy as the war took its toll in their families. Emergency calls always came through my office or apartment, many late at night when I had to arouse sleeping coeds.

Willibald "Bill" Bianchi, class of 1939, the first American honored during World War II non-posthumously, "for conspicuous gallantry and intrepidity above and beyond the call of duty." (1940 Jack Rabbit photo)

On February 26, 1942, Congress announced the awarding of the Congressional Medal of Honor to Willibald "Bill" Bianchi, class of 1939. Bill was a lieutenant in the Philippines when the Japanese attacked the United States in 1941. He managed to silence a Japanese machine gun nest and man an anti-aircraft gun while wounded by two bullets. General Douglas MacArthur awarded the medal "for conspicuous gallantry and intrepidity above and beyond the call of duty." Bill was the first American honored during World War II non-posthumously.

Taken captive when Bataan fell April 9, 1942, Bianchi survived the infamous Bataan death march. Other prisoners told how he moved up and down the line, encouraging those crazed by hunger and thirst. Later in the Japanese camp, he bartered the Japanese guards to get food for

Americans threatened with starvation. On Dec. 15, 1944, he was being transferred from Manila to Japan aboard a Japanese prison ship that sank. Many of those topside were rescued, but Bill was not among them. It was typical; survivors told his family, that Bill had gone into the ship's hold to aid the sick. He was 29 when he died.

Years after the death of her only son, Mrs. Bianchi was working in her home when the felt pad came off the bottom of a candlestick. Willabald had made the candlestick, a gift for his mother, when he was in high school shop class. In a note secreted under the felt, he told his mother that he loved her.

Nowhere was Bianchi more celebrated than in his hometown of New Ulm, Minnesota. In 1955, a new residential street in New Ulm was named Bianchi Drive. South Dakota State College, the "West Point of the Plains" proudly claimed Bianchi as an alumnus, and students talked of his hero-ism. They remembered, too, that he worked his way through college and went out for boxing and football, and the poultry judging team.

Later, Warren Evans, another former State student, had his picture on the cover of *Newsweek* as a Commando in the European Arena. When he returned home, his back was badly scarred from tortures at the hands of the Germans who captured him.

As the war progressed, I received more and more letters from our students in service. I often wondered what the censoring officers thought of those letters addressed to the Dean of Women but containing strange information about the "red haired women" on the Fiji Islands, or sleeping nights on the roof of a Maharajah's palace in India, or their fears of crashing in the Pacific in a B-29. Some of them never made it home. There were 110 former students and one faculty member, an instructor from the English Department, killed in World War II.

STATE'S ARMY AND AIR FORCE GENERALS

Twelve S.D. State alumni, after becoming commissioned officers, have been promoted to the rank of General. Eight of States' Army ROTC commissioned officers later became General officers in the active or reserved forces. Myrna (McCollam) Williamson who graduated in 1960 when women were not allowed into ROTC received a direct commission as a Second Lt. in the Women's Army Corps. Coincidentally, State's ROTC program did commission the first female in the ROTC program in the United States. Additionally, three of States' Air Force ROTC commissioned officers later became General officers in the Air Force.

William E. DePuy graduated from State in 1941 and received an ROTC commission as Second Lt. Infantry. He was promoted to four-star General status in 1973 and was the Commanding General, 1st Infantry Division-Viet Nam. He served as Vice Chief of Staff of the Army and the first commander of the U.S. Army Training and Doctrine Command. As commander he created the mechanisms to restore the Army's self-image as a conventional combat force trained and configured for continental warfare. His plans were the foundation for the training revolution and the development and fielding of the extraordinary combat systems that proved themselves in Operation Desert Storm. Personally, and as the leader of a major Army command, he took hold of a defeated and discouraged Army and put it on the road to victory. He retired in 1977 as the only SDSU alumnus to achieve four star General rank. He was awarded

(left) William E. DePuy, '41—General DePuy was the only SDSU graduate to achieve four star general rank. (right) Myrna Williamson '60—Gen. Williamson was one of the first women ever to be promoted to the rank of general in the U.S. Army. (From SDSU Army ROTC photo collection and the 1940 Jack Rabbit)

an honorary doctorate from SDSU in 1971 and in 1987, the ROTC Building was named DePuy Hall in his honor.

Myrna Williamson graduated from SDSU in 1960. She served a distinguished 28-year career in the staff and command assignments around the world, forging numerous career "firsts." She is the only SDSU female graduate known to achieve the rank of General and was also one of the first women to be promoted to the rank of Brig. Gen. in the United States Army. She retired June 30, 1989, as the senior female General in the United States Army at the time of her retirement.

Seven other State graduates, who started their careers from SDSU Army ROTC, achieved the rank of General of the Army. They are: Maj. Gen. Charles V.Wilson '41, Infantry; Maj. Gen. Alan Nord '52, Air Defense; Lt. Gen. Merle Freitag '62, Transportation Corps; Brig. Gen. Archie Higdon '28, Army Air Corps; Brig. Gen. Don Holiday '50, Field Artillery; Brig. Gen. Robert F. Schulte '59, Armor and Brig. Gen. Jake Krull '60, Field Artillery.

Three of State's graduates who became Air Force commissioned officers have achieved the rank of General: Lt. Gen. Lansford Trapp, Jr., graduated from SDSU in 1969. Maj. Gen. Kurt B. Anderson graduated from SDSU in 1967. Brig. Gen. Thomas Hruby received his Bachelor of Science degree from SDSU in 1968 and a Master of Science degree from SDSU in 1976.

Lt. Gen. Lansford Trapp, Jr., is not only the highest ranking Air Force General who graduated from State but he is also the ranking officer of the Trapp family of S.D. State Air Force officers.

Lansford Trapp Sr., SDSU Math Professor Emeritus, started the Air Force career family tradition in 1940. All five Trapp sons have followed their father's Air Force career path. Collectively the six Trapps have tallied 130 years of proud military serv-

Lt. Gen. Lansford Trapp, Jr. is now the deputy commander of all Air Force units attached to the joint United States Pacific AF Command, Hickman Air Force Base, Hawaii. (Trapp family photo)

ice, logging thousands of hours of flying time. All five sons are SDSU alumni and served as Air Force pilots. All five Trapp sons started their military careers with USAF ROTC commissions from SDSU.

The Trapp family of flyers, from left to right: Steve Trapp, Major, 20 years active duty, USAF Reserve at Luke AFB; Paul Trapp, Lt. Col. USAF, 22 years active duty, Research and Development, Kirtland AFB; Dick Trapp, Lt. Col. Retired, 22 years active duty, USAF Wright Patterson AFB; Lansford Trapp Sr., Lt. Col. USAF Retired, 26 years active duty, Brookings, SD; Mark Trapp, Captain American Airlines, Boca Raton, FL, 9 years active duty USAF; Lansford Trapp Jr., Lt. Gen., 31 years active duty, Deputy Commander, United States Pacific AF Command, Hickham Air Force Base; (Trapp family photo)

WAR-TIME ACTIVITIES

Rev. Leonard Nelson of the Episcopal Church and I had responsibilities for USO dances. And I learned what it was like to be a taxi dancer. Taxi dancers were dance partners for hire. The boys bought tickets and exchanged one ticket for one dance. "Boogie Woogie" was just coming in vogue, and one Italian private, two-thirds my height and width would always seek me out. The officers spent most of their time trying to rescue me from his vigorous routines. The college girls kept their equilibrium quite well, but we encountered problems with the high school girls, who appeared with too much make-up and frequented the streets on the week-ends when the army students were free. They also invaded Pugsley Union in hordes and became a nuisance for the Union Director, especially when there were open houses and they could blend in with the college women.

Dancing so often, I knew every popular tune from "Rosie the Riveter" to smooth dance tunes: "Comin' in on a Wing and a Prayer," "For Me and My Gal," "A Nightingale Sang in Berkeley Square," "White Cliffs of Dover," "Blues in the Night," "When the Lights Go On Again (All Over the World)," "I'll Walk Alone," "I'll be Seeing You," "On the Atchison, Topeka and the Santa Fe," and "Far Away Places."

As rector, Leonard got gasoline rations to give his sermons to the Flandreau Indian School. I was frequently invited to ride with him and his charming wife. Both Leonard and I were devoted to licorice. We would arrive with darkened teeth and dingy mouths, because he somehow managed to produce a yard of black licorice, which we proceeded to devour, somewhat to his wife Marie's disgust. I wondered if the Flandreau girls recognized me as the same person who later talked to them at their "Mother and Daughter" banquet, minus the taint of licorice.

A major from my hometown, Roland Young, who attended high school with me, was assigned to State as the ROTC Adjutant. I had not seen him since he left for Notre Dame for a law degree. He took me to the Army dances and the special dinner dances every three months when a unit graduated. The army took over the Sawnee Hotel for these occasions. The steaks were real, and the talent shows were lively and sophisticated with writers from the *New Yorker*, professional actors and excellent musicians. Roland would take me home early to prevent my seeing too much drinking. My cherub family would congregate at the head of the stairs, and when I said goodnight a whole chorus would chime, "Goodnight, Major." I tried to defuse their interest by explaining that the major was engaged to one of my sister's good friends. He was a wonderful dancer, and he had an endless supply of stories, which became hilarious, as he told them. I enjoyed hearing current information about our classmates at Elgin High, since I had been away from my hometown since the mid-1920s.

SPEECHES AND MORE SPEECHES

Both Dean Brown and President Pugsley had indicated, during my interviews with them before I came to State, that they hoped I would be able to give speeches, as a part of my public relations contribution to student groups, the community and special state conferences. As I had taken some courses in the School of Speech, which were listed on my transcript, I had to admit that I could speak to groups, if the subjects were on national or international affairs.

I had taken speech classes, rather than Liberal Arts, because I thought the faculty was more interesting and the classes were smaller. Consequently my transcript had an impressive list of courses. Some of them, like the History of the Drama, had little to do with public speaking. I even took interpretative dancing under Mrs. Kranz, because of her excellent reputation. I am sure my choreography of a butterfly fluttering over a pool may have looked more like a big brown bear, but I did enjoy the relaxation and body mobility.

After some practical experiences at State, I added topics dealing with college youth, women and my personal philosophies. Had I known initially that I would be deluged with requests, I might have been tempted to develop an annoying mannerism or facial grimace to discourage the rash of speaking engagements. But I was young, earnest and in need of a position. So I promised to speak if any opportunities were offered to me. I did not realize then that I would be haunted by requests, even after my retirement.

METHODISTS AND BAPTISTS

My first summer in Brookings in 1933, Registrar David Doner came to see me and said, "I understand that you are giving the sermon at the Baptist Church next Sunday at eleven o'clock. Will you give the same sermon at the Methodist Church at ten o'clock?" He explained that it would make it possible for their minister to take his family and many children on a trip. He said that the minister had not previously had a vaca-

David B. Doner served as State's Registrar for 44 years from 1918 to 1962. Mr. Doner also served as Alumni Secretary from 1935 until his retirement in 1962. (Instructional Technologies Center photo)

tion, and, besides, the church could not afford to pay a substitute. I reluctantly agreed—another public relations assignment.

Before eleven o'clock, a deacon from the Baptist Church, Dr. Borst, came to Wecota Hall to pick me up. He was unable to locate me and finally sought out Mrs. Gertrude McKnight, my assistant. Dr. Borst said, "Where is that young lady?" To which Mrs. McKnight replied, "She is giving a sermon at the Methodist Church." Dr. Borst was most perturbed and explained that he had made the arrangements himself and how could I be so confused? Mrs. McKnight, with her eyes sparkling, no doubt said, "Oh, she is just practicing her sermon to the Methodists. She knows that she is to speak at the Baptist Church at eleven." Dr. Borst bundled Mrs.

McKnight into his car and drove to the Baptist Church, just in time to see me sprinting frantically the block between the two churches.

But the sequel was the most interesting part of that sermon. Some of the Methodists had been very distressed because the new Dean of Women had talked about communism in the pulpit. My topic had been Religion in the Soviet Union. I really knew quite a lot about this topic because I had studied under Professor Haensel, a Russian refugee at Northwestern for two years, and I had also had a course on Contemporary Russia from Professor Harper at the University of Chicago. The two professors did not always agree. Professor Haensel accused Harper of not telling the whole story because Harper wanted to go back to Russia again for more research. Professor Haensel, on the other hand, had been warned by one of his former Russian students that he was in danger and so he quietly accepted a summer teaching job in Austria. But it took months before his wife and two sons were able to join him, and they lost everything, even his manuscript for a book on The Soviet Economic Planning. Mrs. Haensel's family had considerable property, and her face had the premature lines caused by her unhappy experiences and those of her family. Finally, they were able to come to Evanston, where he assumed his teaching assignment. He had the delightful Old World courtesy and had patiently translated *Izvestia*, *Pravda* and Slavonic periodicals for me. I was working on religion in Russia for an honors course and he was delighted that I had chosen this topic.

Consequently, I did discuss the ideology of Communism: (1) the dictatorship of the Proletariat, (2) the nationalization of wealth and a socialized economy and (3) World Revolution. I also talked about Soviet propaganda against religion, the direct persecution of the Greek Orthodox Church, Soviet substitutes for religion, and a brief history of the old church under the previous czars. This was at the time when the Soviets were renewing their direct persecution of all religions. Previously only the Greek Orthodox Church had suffered. The Soviets were engaging in a gigantic propaganda campaign, including a five-year plan to destroy religion. Even their postage stamps had anti-religious motifs.

The actual situation was certainly serious enough to disturb any Christian church members. The Baptists, however, took the sermon in stride because I had been teaching a Sunday School class on Conflicts of Church and State. I had been promised a post-college age group, but they were mostly past sixty, but they were loyal to their Sunday School teacher. Not so, the Methodists, and I heard about it.

GETTYSBURG SPEECHES

During the height of the dust bowl days, I drove from Brookings to Gettysburg to give three talks. I could see nothing but dust and tumbleweeds across the desolate prairie scene. The drought of the '30s hit western South Dakota the hardest. Those who stayed in the state during the five years of drought were forced to feed Russian thistles to their livestock. Later they saw their cattle, hogs and sheep slaughtered as a part of a livestock reduction plan.

I was scheduled to talk at the Methodist Church, to a men's organization with an Indian name, and at the high school. I had a bad cold and

Drifts of topsoil filled the ditches during the dirty thirties. (Agricultural Heritage Museum photo)

a sinus infection, and the dust made me feel miserable. As I turned north from Blunt I was literally enveloped in a continuous, eerie, cloud of dust. My car lights were of no help, and with the ditches filled with soil, it was almost impossible to discern the road.

Gettysburg had very salty, artesian water, which did nothing for my thirst or morale. The hotel was indeed an experience. Coils of heavy ropes were tied to the steam radiator. I thought workmen had left them. It would never have occurred to me to use the ropes in case of a fire.

It was May 6th, and the birthday of one of our County Agents, who had courted one of the senior women very earnestly during his last year at State. He called the hotel at frequent intervals with inducements for me to come to his birthday party. With each call, a very elderly man would rap on my door and say so-and-so wants to talk to you again, and I followed him downstairs to the telephone. Incidentally, I had a strange feeling that I might be the only guest that night in the hotel. There was no desk in my room, so I curled up on the bed and struggled with my sermon for the Methodists, interrupted at intervals by my friend's insistent invitations, with more and more inducements added as the night wore on. The next morning after my sermon on Hitler and the Church, the first person who introduced herself was the telephone operator. I blanched at the memory of the telephone conversations the night before.

Fortunately for me, some friends rescued me from that hotel on Sunday night. I stayed in a ranch near Hoven, where I had my first and last ride on a tractor. I enjoyed seeing deer in their yard as we feasted on a substantial breakfast to fortify me for my second and third talks.

Speaking in Farm Country

During the mid-'30s and the crisis in Ethiopia, when Italy was determined to end Ethiopia's three thousand years of independence, I was asked to speak on this topic at a session of the Extension Homemakers Conference. Since the Aggie students did not arrive until later, many of the women stayed in Wenona Hall, and I would get to know them quite well.

I planned a rather serious, historical discussion because many people had a very dim and shadowy view of Ethiopia. Some did not know that Abyssinia and Ethiopia were the same country. I discussed the country's geography, military strengths and mostly weaknesses, except for guerrilla tactics; Haile Salassi's rise to power as emperor, the social structure and economic problems, and race and religions, especially the Coptic Church.

Coptic is the Arab term for Egyptian. There were many church buildings, from 1500 to 1800, some built into the rocks. A distinct monastery system in the Abbyssinian church had been founded in the fourth century. The church was an important factor in people's lives. Monophystic Christians, the Coptics, believed in the single composite unconfused nature of Christ and the two natures of humankind, divine and human.

In the middle of this serious discussion in the sunroom of the women's dormitories, a dog entered, sat for a time, yawned very elaborately walked away. I said, "Apparently that Cockerel Spaniel does not appreciate this topic." I thought there were a few more smiles than the situation merited, but then the dog had been rather cute in his actions. A bit later in my discussion of the monasteries I made a flippant remark that nothing female was allowed within the confines of the church property—"not even a female hen." The two bloopers coming so close together were just too much for those good farm women to endure. An epidemic of hearty laughter broke out. Clara Suter, a poultry specialist from Iowa, was literally hanging onto the handles of the French doors convulsed with laughter. When Susan Wilder of the Extension Staff, who had asked me to make the speech, started laughing, all felt free to join her, much to my discomfiture. I did not have the remotest idea of what was amusing them. I gave a hasty look downward to see if any of my lingerie was falling. The more dismayed I looked, the harder they laughed.

Both bloopers had to be explained to me afterwards by Mrs. McKnight. "A cockerel," she said patiently, "is young male domestic fowl. The term for the breed of dog you mentioned is Cocker Spaniel. And as for hens, well, they are all female." The farm women were very gracious afterwards in assuring me that they had appreciated hearing about Ethiopia, in spite of my cockerel and female hen references. I wonder what they said to their local groups later when they reported on the conference.

My lack of knowledge of rural terms was to trouble me quite often. On my first Sunday in Brookings, Herb Cheever, Sr., a lawyer friend of Mrs. McKnight, and his wife took my new assistant and me for a ride. I was intrigued with the names Volga, Sinai, Hayti and the like, but I was startled to notice a sign saying Boars for Sale. My mental picture was one from a grade school geography book, showing wild boars from Borneo with large, curling tusks. My host was amazed and amused by my question of why were there boars in South Dakota? I am certain he retold this yarn many times. I know Mrs. McKnight relished telling it.

On another occasion a friend of mine who owned a farm, had a bunch of posters advertising gilts and boars for sale. Again, I was completely at a loss as to what they were and she, thoroughly diverted, asked if I knew what heifers were.

Heifers I did know about. Years earlier, I went on a research trip to the New Orleans area with Dr. Walter Cox, his wife and another graduate student. In Louisiana at that time, cattle wandered rather carelessly on the highways, and when the topic came up during our drive, Dr. Cox learned that I did not know the term heifer. But neither he, his wife nor the graduate student enlightened me. After our return to Northwestern in the midst of a graduate seminar, Dr. Cox asked me, "By the way, Vivian, have you found out what a heifer is yet?" Of course I had not, but I soon consulted a dictionary. So, I knew about heifers when I arrived in South Dakota.

The Forum

The Forum was a local organization for men, which held monthly dinner meetings in the former guest dining room in the basement of Wenona Hall. Wives were permitted to attend the dinners and hear the speaker, but they were not allowed at that time to take part in the discussions afterward. In spite of these rules, the gentlemen would tolerate a woman speaker, and they invited me to speak in early 1936. Knowing that the group had a generous number of members with Scandinavian backgrounds, I decided to talk about the Nazi infiltration of the three Scandinavian countries. I had read some scholarly articles on the subject and arranged an inter-library loan for some books from the University of Chicago, including one called *"Rats in the Larder"* by Joachim Joesten, which was a study of Nazi influence in Denmark.

A cornerstone of the Nazi credo was a mystic belief in the superiority of the Nordic race. The most authoritative dogmatists of the Nazi creed repeatedly pointed to Scandinavia as the home of the glorious Nordic race.

I pointed out that it was impossible to believe that the Nordic dreamworld of the Nazis could ever coincide with the Nordic conception of life. Scandinavians are individualist to the core and democrats by military rule tradition. They were utterly opposed to the authoritarian leader principle of the totalitarian Third Reich. They despised the Nazi attitude toward women, whose role was to be limited to the kitchen, their children and the church. Peace, freedom, progress and democracy—those four words absolutely outlawed in the Reich—covered the Scandinavian world order. The Nazi suitors were dauntless, but their efforts fell on comparatively barren soil. There was no lost war, no mass misery, no disgruntled middle class, no Jewish population and no threat of Bolshevism. A succession of splits, fusions, scandals and unpleasant disclosures discredited these indigenous groups in the public eye.

Much, much more serious were the German Nazi organizations in Scandinavia. In each country the local leaders were placed under a German leader. The Nazi parties in Scandinavia were under a peculiar Nazi organization called the Nordic Society. Hitler's most prominent advisers were members of its executive body. The organization was well financed and sent out lecturers, agitators and propagandists by the hundreds.

I really felt well prepared on this subject, but the affect on my audience was complete incredulity. Where did I get all this rubbish and propaganda? They accused me of sheer sensationalism. I was utterly crushed as I weakly explained that I had read the material in scholarly sources.

Years later, as the events unfolded in Germany, and Hitler's legions absorbed Denmark and Norway, I was credited with clairvoyant powers. How did I know that the names I had mentioned in 1936 would be prominent in the news later? I can still recall Dr. Hume and Dr. Hutton talking about my speech and how I had anticipated the dangers. So my reputation for understanding the international scene grew suddenly and rather startlingly—but I paid a price earlier! Incidentally, the wives had a much more favorable reaction in personal comments after my talk, although they were not allowed to take part in the Forum discussion.

KIWANIANS

During the height of the Suez Crisis in the mid-1970s, Bill McCann asked me to speak to the local Kiwanis Club about Egypt. As I was introduced and rose to speak, I suddenly saw three Egyptian students seated in the audience. I knew that they were scheduled to leave for Egypt that very week. I had to quickly revise my criticisms of Egypt in order to not offend our three guests, who became quite volatile and heated when they discussed the crisis in their country. My talk was mild, non-abrasive, and almost worthless, I might add, after all my censoring. In the discussions following my talk, they amazed the Kiwanians by insisting that the British used poison gas (mustard gas) at Port Said, along with other allegations. But at least I did not incite their comments.

Afterwards I berated Bill McCann for bringing the Egyptians as guests and forcing me to change most of my speech. He replied, "I was so sick of their side of the story that I wanted them to hear the straight story from you." Later that same evening, the Egyptian students sat near me at a banquet and they were very friendly, due to my anemic talk earlier in the day. Public relations won at the expense of the historian, but they went home without blaming our institution or the Dean of Women for making bitter criticisms of their country.

At various times and under different programs, State has had groups of international students as guests or regular students on our campus. As adviser to the International Relations Club, I had the pleasure of many contacts with them. As a history professor, I was often asked to speak to their group.

TEACHERS INSTITUTE

Once when Dr. Harold Crothers was Acting President, he asked if I would give a couple of talks daily for 10 days at a Teachers Institute series before the opening of college.

He thought the places where I would be speaking would be new to me and that it would be good public relations for the college. I agreed and took my sister along. I spoke on an international topic in the morning and on a personal philosophy in the afternoon. The itinerary included Ipswich, Leola, Selby, Faulkton, Timber Lake, Dupree, Mobridge, McIntosh and McLaughlin.

I shared speaking responsibilities with a Salvation Army Captain from Aberdeen and Mr. Bill Thompson from the State Department of Education. Before the circuit was finished we could easily have given each other's talks. Since

Harold Crothers served as Dean of Engineering for 30 years from 1925 to 1955 and Acting President from 1946 to 1947 and again from 1957 to 1958. (Instructional Technologies Center photo)

the Salvation Army Captain had to return nightly to his base at Aberdeen, we switched our speeches to accommodate his schedule. My sister Olive and I drove extra long distances in order to enjoy good hotels in Aberdeen, Mobridge and Selby. When Mr. Thompson found out that we were apprehensive about the distances involved, he offered to follow us, so that we would not need to worry.

We had entirely too much excitement on Saturday night in Selby. It was at the time of interest in oil developments in the area, and luxury cars with Texas license plates were everywhere. Failing to get any sleep that night because of noise and loud music, we decided to attend the Methodist Church the next morning for spiritual restoration. After the service, we explored our hotel to find out where the night-long entertainment had taken place. The restaurant section was quite small, but the bar was enormous by comparison. Fortunately, there were no sensational newspaper articles featuring Big Foot roaming in the McIntosh-McLaughlin area to frighten us at the time we were there.

The questions and discussions after my talk on the international scene were very revealing. The rural teachers were wholesome, sincere and earnest, but many were inadequately prepared. I understood why some of our students from rural areas struggled hopelessly with English requirements upon entering college. I remember one good story told by a superintendent. A small boy came home jubilantly saying that he would not have to go to school for several days because his teacher was going on an "innocent toot," his term for institute.

I profited from my rural circuit by seeing many small communities. There had been adequate rainfall late that summer, and the beauty of the area was incredible and so unexpected. Later, some of those rural teachers turned up in my summer classes. Incidentally, some of the local newspaper accounts of my talks were amazing. I found myself often wondering, "Oh, is that what I said?" Altogether, it was a unique experience.

HEREFORD AND BLACK ANGUS BREEDERS

After my confessions of my lack of knowledge of rural terms, my friends were surprised to learn that I have spoken to groups like the Hereford and Black Angus breeders—not at the same time, of course, because each group is convinced of the superiority of the breed they raise. I must hasten to add, however, that my topics were on the international scene, areas where I hoped I had some expertise.

Because of a talk I made to a women's club, the wife of a Hereford breeder near Britton persuaded her husband to ask me to speak at the state meeting of Hereford breeders in the late 1950s. As my sister and I were enjoying the hilly countryside on the road near Britton, we suddenly found ourselves in the midst of a sea of cattle. Paranoid with fear, I violently honked the car horn, but it only provoked placid, bovine stares and not an acceleration of their pace in crossing the road. Suddenly, too, I was struck with a new worry—suppose a bull suddenly resented the color of my red Mercury. The herd continued to cross the highway six to eight abreast very leisurely, and there was not a soul in sight, only cattle. I worried, too, that another car might come over the hill too fast to stop for the cattle blockade. The minutes passed, and it was getting perilously close to my speaking commitment. Finally, after what seemed an eternity to me, they all crossed the road and a lone horseback rider, waved and smiled as he crossed in front of my car. I drove off to my appointment with the Hereford breeders, thinking some very unkind thoughts about their animals.

Later I spoke to a Black Angus Breeders State Meeting in Watertown. There were pictures of Black Angus used as place cards, so I saw what they looked like—more forbidding than the Herefords I had encountered.

The men sang a robust song about a little Black Angus bull that does this and that, but they substituted a lot of la-la-las, obviously censoring themselves for my benefit. I did not confess to the Black Angus breeders that I had ever had anything to do with the Hereford breeders! The Director of our Experiment Station had been responsible for this assignment.

WEBSTER

For three years in a row I was asked to speak to the high school seniors in Webster at a banquet, sponsored by the Business and Professional Women. Each time we were guests in the home of the sheriff and heard some weird radio calls all night. On the third trip I suggested that some of our sister institutions might object to my having a monopoly on contacting their high school women, but I did thoroughly enjoy my visits there and their delightful hospitality.

I did return again to Webster to speak at ladies' night, for the Kiwanians. State has some splendid Alumni supporters in Webster. The women in Webster were surprised that I had not met a handsome young man, an ex-auctioneer, who was attending State. His name was Frank Denholm. I told them that I did know his brother, Robert, very well and had spent hours counseling him to take advanced work in Hospital Administration at my alma mater. Robert became a very successful hospital administrator in Denver until his untimely death. His wife and daughter are both nurses.

TORONTO-ASTORIA

During the Second World War one could obtain extra gasoline for official duties, like giving commencement speeches.

I invited three faculty women and a young engineering student, Junis Storry, who later became Dean of Engineering at State.

His sister was in the graduating class at Astoria. And what a ride! There were road repairs, a terrific spring thunderstorm, and finally trouble with something in the gas line. Twice, Junis disconnected the gas line and sucked out the gas, hoping to dislodge the offending object, while I fumed, "Spit it all out, or you will be poisoned." He was dressed in his Sunday best, and was getting wet, besides flirting with his life by gulping the gasoline.

Finally, we arrived at the high school, and I ran from the car to give the talk, while my friends sought out a garage to repair the gas line. I was late, tense and very upset. Climbing the steps to the stage I hit my head quite violently on a support for a false ceiling, installed as a

Junis Storry was on the Electrical Engineering staff from 1965 to 1972, Dean of Engineering from 1972 to 1982 and Distinguished Professor of Engineering from 1982 to 1985. (Instructional Technologies Center photo)

prop for the senior play. The superintendent had forgotten to warn me. Despite a throbbing headache and fragile, nervous condition, I was determined to deliver the speech. As the storm continued to rage, the lights flickered in and out. Once I noticed that my friends were back when the lights came on again. Then, after another interval of darkness, the lights revealed a young woman nursing her baby in the front row—a sight that momentarily numbed my thinking, but I recovered and continued.

A year later I was invited to give Memorial Day speeches to the towns of Toronto and Astoria. Again there were road repairs and detours. I missed the 10 a.m. speech and a dinner. I had tried to find the home of my hosts without success, only to learn that I was in Hendricks and not Toronto. When I finally arrived in Astoria very late, I was whisked into a car and taken to the cemetery for a 3 p.m. speech, and I was equally harried as the year before. Two such experiences in the Toronto-Astoria area were enough.

HAZARDS OF SPEECH GIVING

I grew so tired of road construction that I was always glad when I could reach my speaking engagements via the Chicago & North Western railroad line. I could stay overnight and return by train the next day, even though it meant a loss of time. The train was my only means of travel during winter months, with the unpredictable South Dakota weather.

Those depots, with their potbellied stoves, always had a unique smell. I wondered where it came from. The station agent, wearing a green eyeshade, clicked the Morse code messages to remote areas, from the bay window where he could watch both ways. Invariably, the seats snagged my nylon hose. At night in small towns, I was frequently the only passenger waiting for the train.

The Dean of Women was called the Guiding Light in the 1953 Jack Rabbit. (1953 Jack Rabbit photo)

The high school commencement season usually coincides with our violent spring thunderstorms, and I have never been comfortable driving at night alone. Consequently, I usually invited friends to keep me company. On one occasion I planned to arrive at Lake Benton with my guests one half hour ahead of time, so that we could enjoy looking at the lake. As we turned toward the hill, where the high school is located, we saw a terrific congestion of parked cars, and one of my friends said, "Did you know Minnesota has daylight savings time?" I had forgotten and was a half-hour late. The eighth graders and high school graduates were weary of waiting outside, and I tried to gain my composure by remarking that South Dakota did not tamper with God's time. The superintendent apologized for not reminding me of the time change.

The acoustics were usually bad in those stuffy auditoriums. I always had to use my full vocal volume to drown out the confusion of a small fry walking down the aisle or a wailing baby. The crowds always overflowed the space. The local awards, honors and student talent inevitably consumed a large chunk of time, while the speaker was left to fidget in an uncomfortable folding chair under the hot lights on the platform, trying to look reasonably interested. If I was feeling fidgety, it was no wonder that the children got restless by the time I was introduced.

Some of the introductions were astonishing. I felt somehow that I was supposed to be very flattered for the privilege of speaking in a domain usually reserved for men. And I worked very hard on those commencement talks, preaching the message of the need for higher education, especially for women.

Conservative fathers were inclined to give their young men preference during the times of economic hardship. How often I repeated the phrase, "When you educate a woman, you educate an entire family."

Speaking on current international topics had its inherent hazards. A crisis could develop between the interval of my acceptance and the time I finally gave the talk.

On March 10, 1948, I was scheduled to give a talk on Czechoslovakia to the Pi Gamma Mu organization at noon. Just before my 11 a.m. class on Contemporary Europe, two of my students came dashing in to tell me that Jan Masaryk was dead. Masaryk was the Minister of Foreign Affairs of the Czechoslovak Republic, son of Thomas Garrigue Masaryk, the President-Liberator, founder of the Czechoslovak State. The radio reported that a single light was burning early in the morning at the Czeznine Palace in the fourth floor private apartment where Masaryk lived. The bathroom window was open, and a corpse lay on the paving streets below. The radio report indicated there were no signs of a struggle at the scene.

At the Pi Gamma Mu luncheon, no one apparently had heard the radio report, so my news startled them. I went on to explain that just two weeks earlier Masaryk had seen the parliamentary liberties of the Czechoslovak nation destroyed. Did he commit suicide by jumping out of the window, to show his feeling that the situation was hopeless, or did someone push him out of the window? The verdict is still not in, but most historical critics felt that his suicide was a confession of the hopeless position of his beloved country. We may never know the true circumstances of his death, as the doctor who attended him died a few months thereafter while in police custody.

After Russia launched Sputnik in the 1950s, I received a rash of requests to speak. Since it was an excellent opportunity to emphasize the need for more studies of engineering, mathematics and science in higher education, I carried the message as well as a discussion of the current relations between the Soviet Union and the United States. Little did I know my comments might be viewed as incendiary. At a Rural Electrification meeting in Minnesota, for instance, the first question a farmer asked me at the discussion period was, "Are you a Russian?" I explained that I was half-German and half-French, and that my parents were born in the United States. Placated, he proceeded to ask another question.

After I gave a talk at an American Association of University Women meeting in Huron, the organization's president admitted to me that she had been afraid the meeting would be disrupted by a demonstration. It failed to materialize, but her comments still gave me a jolt. Was it dangerous to speak on Russia in South Dakota? Or were my speeches more influential than I ever suspected? I had given a radio interview earlier, but it was certainly not the kind to kindle a demonstration, or so I thought.

SOUTH DAKOTA ART MUSEUM

One of my private hopes as I gave dozens and dozens of speeches to women's clubs throughout the state was that I would somehow influence the vote on the final location of the South Dakota Art Museum.

South Dakota Memorial Art Center shortly after construction and before it was re-named the South Dakota Art Museum (Agricultural Heritage Museum photo)

I'll never know if I had any influence, but I'm so pleased to have the Art Museum on our campus, where it has greatly enriched the cultural program of the University and the community. The Harvey Dunn paintings of South Dakota pioneers and scenes and the famous and exquisite Marghab linens have become an important tourist attraction. I'm certain that State's large collection of Harvey Dunn paintings, which President Fred Leinbach was instrumental in obtaining, was a far more important factor in the vote to locate the Museum here.

Before it opened, the Harvey Dunn paintings were displayed in Pugsley Union and carefully watched

Fred Leinbach served as State's President from 1946 to 1951. (Instructional Technologies Center photo)

by the Union Director, Harlan Olson. Robert Karolevitz, one of our alumni and a talented student of mine, has written a biography, entitled, "Where Your Heart Is—The Story of Harvey Dunn." Incidentally, I also have a copy of one of Bob Karolevitz's early publications, a song titled, "Does No Mean No?" He wrote the music and words and published it in Hollywood in 1946. He sent a copy to me with a note that read, "Not Gershwin, nor Mercer, cuz gosh...it's much worser." Since then he has researched and written a shelf full of books.

The Cord and Tassel linen design, part of the world famous Vera Marghab embroidered linen collection housed in the South Dakota Art Museum. (South Dakota Art Museum photo by Alexis Xenakis)

The Marghab Gallery at the South Dakota Art Museum first opened in November 1970, featuring embroidered designs by Vera Way Marghab, a Watertown, S.D. native.

The pieces, embroidered by hand on linen and Margandie, were designed as backgrounds for china, silver and crystal. The size of the collection made it impossible to display all at once. The collection was a spectacular gift to the people of South Dakota and to State.

ON CAMPUS SPEECHES

I know that speaking to so many campus student organizations each year has enriched my life and helped me immensely in my role as a counselor simply because the students knew me and did not hesitate to consult me about their problems. Teaching Contemporary World History also helped me as a counselor, because my students had confidence in me as a teacher first, and secondly as a Dean of Women. Frequently, they told me of a friend who needed my help. A few years back, I received a copy of a delightful historical novel by one of my former students and Sigma members with an autograph reading, "With warm memories of your inspiring teaching." The book is sophisticated and well researched . I feel a certain vicarious pleasure as I proudly read it.

President John Headley asked me to give my first commencement address to State.

I used the topic "The Fourth Freedom"—freedom from fear. This was one of the four fears used as a slogan during World War II.

My second commencement talk came as a request from President Briggs in December of 1972. It was the last time the exercises were to be held in the Old Barn. My topic was: "From Memory Lane to Horizons Unlimited." If you do not like "The Winds of Change," please blame Dr. Briggs and Dean Allen Barnes, who persuaded me that I should write about the days that are no more. Here I am, in my nineties, still struggling to finish this book, while my alumni friends are becoming impatient with the delay.

John Headley was President at State from 1951 to 1958. (Instructional Technologies Center photo)

THE RIGHT KIND OF YOUNG PEOPLE
AND
UNFORGETTABLE WOMEN

I would rather work with college students than with any other segment of society. Although the faculty makes crucial contributions to the running of a university, it is still the vibrant energy of the students that gives the institution its life and traditions. It was thrilling for me to work with these marvelous, aspiring young people for more than 40 years as Dean of Women and Professor of History. Students are the *raison d'être* (reason for being) of an educational institution.

Nineteenth century graduates returning to State today would find no surviving buildings from their era. Their traditions, too, of literary societies and YMCA activities, are long gone. Over the years, students have staged a variety of special events, only some became traditions that are still observed today. Other traditions, cherished for a short time, served their purpose and passed into oblivion. With over 200 student organizations on our campus today, new traditions are developing rapidly, along with changing attitudes of what is relevant for today's students and the role of the University. The winds of tradition are capricious.

When I arrived on this campus in the fall of 1932, I was far from a militant feminist, but I became concerned immediately about improving the scholastic standards, social life and role of women students on a campus where men dominated by a ratio of three to one. In the process I was responsible for stimulating a large number of new traditions, some of which became lost but served the purpose at the time they were developed and enthusiastically carried out by the students.

THE AMERICAN ASSOCIATION OF UNIVERSITY WOMEN

I was terribly disappointed when I discovered in the fall of 1932 that our women graduates could not become full members of the American Association of University Women. One of my first goals was to obtain accreditation for State by this important and prestigious organization. I learned this was a critical first step for my long-term emphasis of raising

Dean Volstorff congratulates and welcomes new members into Alpha Lambda Delta, Freshmen women's Honorary. (1968 Jack Rabbit photo)

the standards and recognition of women scholars through such organizations as Alpha Lambda Delta, which is the national freshmen honor society for freshmen women, and a chapter of Mortar Board, the national honor organization for senior women. It took two decades of dedicated efforts to obtain the accreditation of State by the American Association of University Women. A chapter of Alpha Lambda Delta was established at SDSU on April 21, 1968, and the Sigma Lambda Sigma chapter of Mortar Board was installed at SDSU on April 30, 1972, just before my retirement in 1973.

Since my retirement, the national organizations of both Alpha Lambda Delta and Mortar Board, have become coed organizations.

The road to accreditation was difficult. It began in the spring of 1936, right as I was planning to attend the national convention of the National Association of Deans of Women in New Orleans at my own expense. I had done much of my research for my doctoral dissertation on Louisiana Gov. W.C.C. Claiborne, and the Louisiana Historical Association was interested in publishing my dissertation as a biography, a project I never had the opportunity to complete. I was thoroughly absorbed in making my plans for the trip when I received a call to see President Pugsley, who wanted me to go to the Convention of the American Association of University Women in Savannah, Ga., instead of the dean's convention in New Orleans. He wanted me to find out what our institution had to do to become accredited. Since it was one of my major goals, I could scarcely refuse.

On a personal level, the trip was delightful. My sister, who was living in Elgin, Ill., joined me, and we enjoyed the southern hospitality of an AAUW member's home in Savannah, because we were too late to get hotel reservations. We drove to Savannah in my new car, and I remember many courteous service station attendants who helped out by telling us of the newest motels or hotels, providing lotion for my badly sunburned left arm and whisk brooms to dust out the floor of the car, and even warning us in Tennessee about a tornado and pleading for us to not travel any later in the mountains. A South Dakota license brought the reaction that we must be innocent and, therefore, naive about mountain driving. It was my first car, and my first experience in mountain driving, so the warning was much appreciated.

I was appalled, however, by the magnitude of the problems our institution faced before we could be considered for AAUW accreditation. I had an interview with a member of the accreditation committee and learned that most of the changes we needed to make would require time and money, despite our tight financial circumstances and my sense of urgency to make progress. The list was long: more women on our faculty with doctorate degrees, higher salaries, more women on policy-making committees, more liberal arts courses and majors such as art, speech and music, better health care for women, an expanded physical education program for women, more professional and honor societies for women, and more activities to develop student leadership. The AAUW committee also was concerned about our crowded departments, heavy teaching loads and the absence of an adequate retirement policy.

My only hope for reducing some of the obstacles to achieving accreditation lay in improving female students' scholarship, adding more professional organizations for women and developing student leadership through a broader program of activities. I went to work on these problems and in the process introduced new traditions: Freshmen cozies, Freshmen lectures on social behavior, the Coed Ball, Senior Matinee Tea Dances, Women's Day, open houses, formal faculty teas, and a host of new organizations including: Angel Flight, Theta Sigma Phi (Journalism), Kappa Epsilon (Pharmacy), University Dames, International Relations

Dean Volstorff greets WSGA (Women's Self Governing Association) members. (1949 Jack Rabbit photo)

Club (with the help of Professor Harding), and finally the two national Greek social sororities: Chi Omega and Alpha Xi Delta.

Meanwhile, President Pugsley was preoccupied with three building projects: a student union, men's dormitory and an annex to Wecota Hall. His bout with cancer caused serious illness and, finally, his resignation. Dr. George Brown became the interim acting president until Dr. Lyman Jackson arrived. President Jackson's regime was absorbed with the war programs on campus, and AAUW affairs were put on the back burner. After President Jackson, Dr. Harold Crothers became acting president until Dr. Fred Leinbach came to State.

For the first time in years I felt that I must urge the new president to consider the importance of AAUW accreditation and make some real progress on my goal. I will admit to pushing him hard, and he was sympathetic to helping resolve the problems. He did secure salary increases for women (and men), employ more women faculty with doctorate degrees, and appoint more women to important committees.

In June of 1949 I went to the AAUW convention in Seattle, hoping for some real progress, as Dr. Anna Hawkes was the incoming AAUW president. I knew her through my work in the National Association of

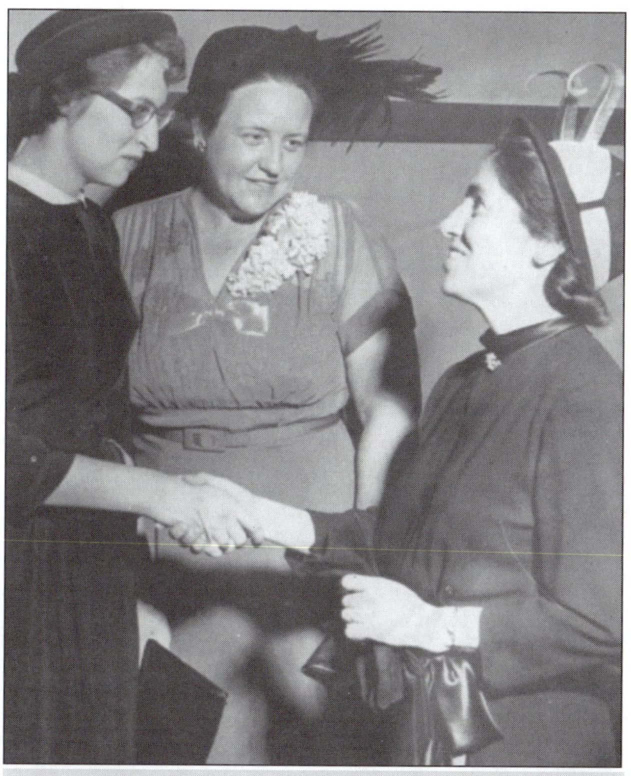

Ms. Leinbach greets Anna Rose Hawkes, incoming AAUW president, during her 1949 AAUW related visit. (1950 Jack Rabbit photo)

Women Deans and Counselors when she was president of that organization. We did make real progress! She agreed to try to attend our fall AAUW workshop in Pierre, visit Augustana College, and then come to State. She knew how long I had worked to achieve accreditation and was sympathetic. She ended up spending over a day with us, and I even had to find some pheasant for her to sample before she left. Luckily, Nell Kendall had some frozen in her refrigerator.

President Leinbach attended all of her discussions and even asked to be included in a coffee session at Moriarty's late at night before she left. Somehow, I cannot remember how, I became involved in a wager with Dr. Leinbach for me to lose 25 pounds by the end of the following March. To get AAUW accreditation I was willing to do almost anything.

I won the bet by nibbling on endless vegetable and fruit meals at the old Pugsley Union. The wager vastly amused Dr. Hawkes, but she liked President Leinbach, and the feeling was mutual. The result of my wager now resides in the University Union ballroom—a Steinway grand piano. Dr. Joseph Moisan, a former Union Director, had the piano refinished and repaired when the new Union ballroom was named after me in 1974.

After Dr. Hawkes' visit in 1949, there followed months of tedious assembling of pertinent information for the AAUW accreditation committee. Home Economics Professor Alice Rosenberger and I spent our Sunday afternoons together for weeks and weeks, getting the materials in order. Registrar David Doner threatened to give me a desk in his department, since I was constantly bothering his staff for information.

Dean of Arts and Science, Frank Schultz, was very helpful in allowing his secretary to make the numerous copies of our report to the accreditation committee in 1950. All of the efforts since 1932 finally cul-

AAUW plaque and 11/15/81 dedication To Quality Education for One Century, Honoring Women Educators. Left to right: Margaret Fishback, Brookings Women's Club; Ruth Redhead, AAUW Committee; Jean Walz, AAUW Committee; Vivian Volstorff, AAUW Committee Chair; Elizabeth Berg, AAUW Brookings, Chair and Sherwood Berg, SDSU President. (Briggs Library photo)

minated with the accreditation award. The efforts were well worthwhile. Now our women graduates can enjoy membership in an organization dedicated to scholarship, both nationally and internationally. AAUW is one organization whose members belong to all the professions and who believe in the continued intellectual growth of its members, through study of national and international issues. Through the efforts of the Brookings Branch of AAUW, a memorial plaque, bearing the University's Centennial logo, was dedicated to "the women who contributed to a century of quality education" at South Dakota State University. The dedication in November of 1981 was held in the Briggs Library with appropriate ceremonies.

State has had a large number of outstanding women educators who remained loyal through years in spite of constant financial hardships and miserable weather conditions.

ALPHA LAMBDA DELTA AND MORTAR BOARD

The next accomplishments, obtaining chapters of Alpha Lambda Delta and Mortar Board, would not have been possible without the years and years of efforts by successive groups of Sigma Lambda Sigma members, a social senior honor organization. These unpaid senior counselors generously contributed their time and talents to help improve the status of women on our campus and tackled numerous new projects with enthusiasm and ingenuity. I hope that as alumnae they felt that their efforts were worthwhile. No other single organization was as helpful to me in planning new programs and projects for the benefit of our women students. Current members of Mortar Board will have a hard time measuring up to the high Sigma standards of scholarship, leadership and service.

Sigma Lambda Sigma has been in existence at South Dakota State since the spring of 1930 as an honor society for senior women. When I became the adviser to the group in the fall of 1932, the major project of the organization was the spring May Day, held in the Sylvan Theatre to honor the May queen, two maids of honor and eight class attendants. Freshmen women danced in the May Pole dances, while junior women carrying the daisy chain were masked with a golden mask as pledges. All the women students on campus selected the queen and her court. The State College Band added glamour to the program by an interpretative dance with a yearly theme and music.

Women's Day Banquet 1934. (Volstorff photo collection)

In 1934, Sigma started Women's Day as an effort to recognize outstanding women scholars and leaders on our very masculine campus. A Women's Day assembly, which honored the outstanding freshmen women scholars, preceded the May Day event. The all-women's chorus, Pasquettes, named after our South Dakota state flower, and the Faculty Women's Chorus under the direction of Mrs. Lyman Jackson frequently sang during this assembly. A luncheon was added for Sigma actives and their mothers, and a banquet was held in the evening for women students, their mothers and the faculty. Scholarships from all divisions, departments and organizations were awarded at the banquet, including the Sigma Lambda Sigma scholarship to the highest-ranking freshman woman.

The practice of granting this scholarship continued until 1973. The *Collegian* was ably edited on this day by an all-women staff who published several news stories about freshmen scholars, Sigma pledges, scholarship winners and the identity of the May Queen and her court. All college women wore white dresses on Women's Day as a part of the tradition.

In the early years, Women's Day banquet speakers consisted of a woman faculty member, an alumna of Sigma and a representative of each class. Miss Gertrude Young, Mrs. Earl Serles and several Deans of Women from neighboring institutions served as speakers. I usually gave a brief history of the traditions and program of Sigma at the end. Each

1956 Women's Day May Pole Dance. (Agricultural Heritage Museum photo)

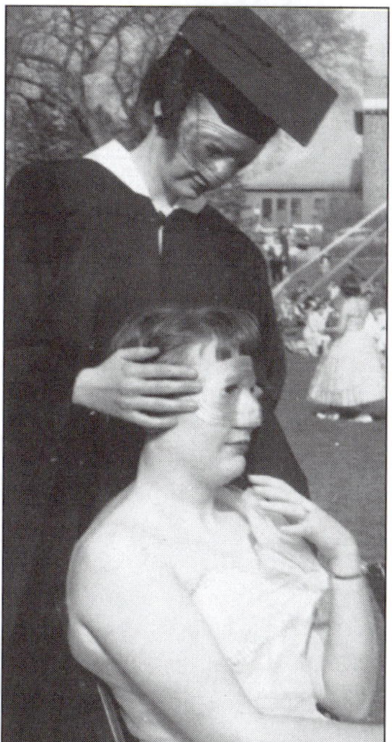

Sigma members garbed in black gowns put the finger and mask on new Sigma pledges. (1957 Jack Rabbit photo)

1932 Women's Day Queen. (1933 Jack Rabbit photo)

Alpha Lambda Delta key in Student Union Crest Room. SDSU Chapter of this Freshmen Women's Honor Society was approved on April 21, 1968. The organization is now coed. (J. O. Pedersen photo)

year, Sigma selected a theme for the banquet, and frequently the class representatives proved to be the most interesting speakers. All speeches were kept very brief to give time for the many scholarship awards.

In later years, parents were invited to the Women's Day Banquet, and with the advent of the Harding distinguished lectures, we were able to utilize such outstanding speakers as Mrs. Patsy Takemoto Mink, (U.S. Representative), Nila Magidoff (Russian born refugee writer), Ramona Ripston (ACLU of Southern California), Audrey Rowe Colom (women's activist) and Betty Friedan (author, feminist)

Many services and projects were carried out by Sigma members in the years prior to World War II and during the war. Activities included: acting as unpaid senior counselors to freshmen women, helping me to arrange faculty-student forums on Sunday evenings in faculty homes prior to the construction of Pugsley Union, assisting with U.S.O. dances and programs during the war for the 1,800 Army and Air Force units stationed on our campus, suggesting free programs on ballroom dancing and bridge instruction to the Board of Control and later to the Union Board, stimulating a University-wide tutoring service. They also served as hostesses at special events like Jackrabbit Round-Up for high school seniors, Scholar's Day and Parents' Day. One group sponsored a Mistletoe formal ball at the holiday season, which was very successful but a tremendous burden for eight or nine women to sponsor. The ball was discontinued because the risk of financial loss was considered too grave at the time with the limited number of men on campus. Also, Sigma members did not want to put Women's Day in jeopardy. From the fall of 1932 until my retirement in 1973, Sigma members also assisted me with my informal fireside cozies for freshmen women and new transfers. Sigma members have always published the *Golden Mask*, a newsletter for alumnae of Sigma, containing significant feature stories about campus changes, new buildings, new programs and faculty, and students who have received special honors.

After months of correspondence, in October of 1967 Sigma paid the charter fee for a chapter of Alpha Lambda Delta, which was installed on April 21, 1968.

By the fall of 1969 "Women's Lib" became a new movement on campus and all students sought relevancy and identity in new ways. May Queens and beauty pageants were frowned upon. In the process, Women's Day activities were abandoned. Starting in 1970 Sigma sponsored annual one-day symposiums on topics such as "Human Sexuality" and "Women's Liberation," and co-sponsored with the Native American Club an "Indian Awareness Week" in March of 1972. We had some very controversial speakers with the winds of change. In particular, the transition from the sedate Women's Day to a symposium on human sexuality, with an absent speaker who was incarcerated in Massachusetts because of an illegal display of contraceptives, created quite a whirlwind. Instead of a keynote address, we had to be content with students from a Minneapolis college, who discussed coed residence halls and the attendant results. Our students were fascinated with such potential freedom for living and visitations.

Finally in September of 1971 we received word that the National Council of Mortar Board had approved our application to National

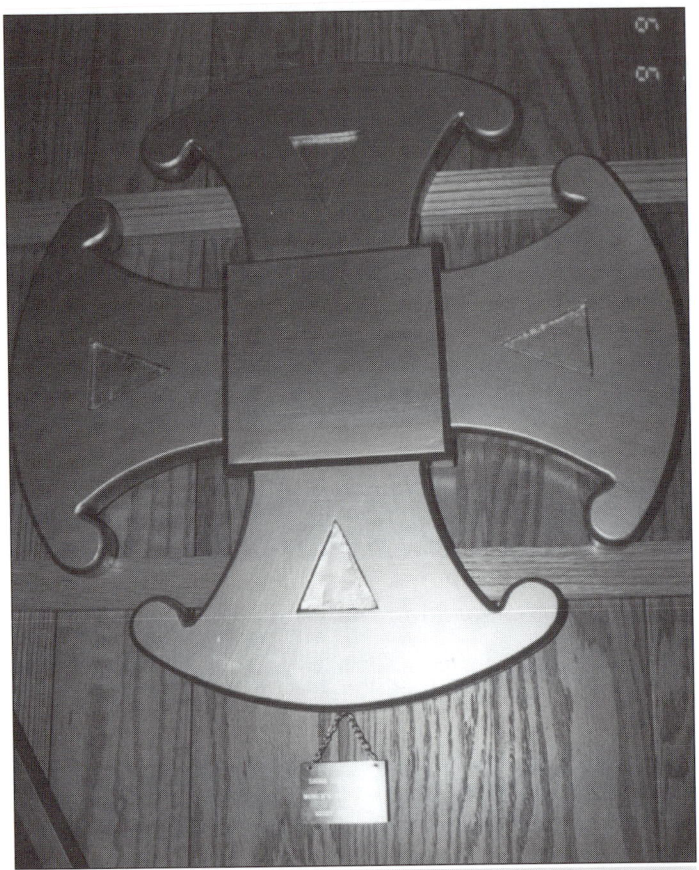

Sigma Lambda Sigma key in Student Union Crest Room. Sigma Lambda Sigma is the SDSU Chapter, the 151st Chapter of Mortar Board, was installed at SDSU on April 13, 1972. (J.O. Pedersen photo)

Mortar Board, subject to the approval of the chapters in Section XVI. Mrs. Jayne Wade Anderson, our charming installing officer and national treasurer of Mortar Board, had visited our campus the previous year. We were very grateful to her for her favorable report, which made installation possible on April 13, 1972. Ours was the 151st chapter.

Representatives from chapters at the University of North Dakota, North Dakota State University and the University of South Dakota were present at our installation service.

Finally my three dreams were fulfilled realities!

The Right Kind Of Young People

With the beginning of Mortar Board came the end of the Sigma honor society. Gone forever were May Pole Dances and May Queens processions in the Sylvan Theatre. Gone, too, were sunrise initiation services for Sigma pledges in the president's garden, with the aroma of flowers refreshed by the morning dew and the pleasant chirping of the birds. While Mrs. Pugsley was first lady, and an honorary member of Sigma, the installation breakfast was held in the president's home with elaborate table decorations made by the artistic hostess. With the opening of the Pugsley Union, the breakfasts were held there, with an individual rose or corsage substituted for the previous elaborate table decorations. Our chapter of Mortar Board is the Sigma Lambda Sigma chapter, perpetuating the name of a great organization of truly talented young women. Sharing in the exploration of the latent talents and potentials of another human being can be a wonderfully rewarding profession. To be successful you must believe that there is a touch of the divine in everyone. If you are patient, sensitive, discerning, and learn how to listen, you will be successful in finding that precious talent or quality in another, which you can genuinely admire. You can never pretend to be interested. Students, no matter how upset, can detect instantly if you are sincere or just feigning an interest in their problems. After problems were solved and a real basis of friendship and trust had been mutually reached, I would ask the student to help other girls, or get them to me or someone else for help. The result was a ripple affect. Soon a whole group of my reformed or transformed counselees were dedicated to helping others to avoid their mistakes. That is the greatest satisfaction a counselor or administrator can experience.

Mortar Board today continues to encourage the development of precious young talent. At the national level the focus continues to be academic excellence, leadership, scholarship and community service. The current Mortar Board national goal is "Reading is Leading." SDSU members of Mortar Board are volunteering in Brookings Elementary Schools, where they are helping youth to become superior readers.

Students helping students leads to many wonderful and rewarding outcomes. It is truly amazing how many young people themselves ignore talent until someone encourages them to find their identity, their confi-

(1999)

Club provides great opportunity for students

Local Mortar Board stress national theme of "Reading is Leading"

BY RACHEL DALY
Collegain Reporter

Mortar Board is a national organization that stresses academic excellence, leadership, scholarships and community service.

Ryan Boekelheide, president of the Brookings Mortar Board Chapter, attended a conference in Columbus, Ohio in mid-July. Chapters from across the country sent one student representatives to the conference. Students discussed ideas such as the organization's national theme.

They decided on "Reading is Leading."

"Mainly our goal is to carry out the national theme and gain public awareness," Boedelheide said.

The Brookings Chapter has been fulfilling their obligation by volunteering at Hillcrest Elementary School, where members have helped students with reading, homework and tests.

Kara Karmody, an SDSU health promotions student, sees great value in the program.

> **"***It's an honor to be a part of Mortar Board.***"**
>
> **KARA KARMODY,**
> health promotions student

"It's an honor to be a part of Mortar Board," she said. "They have a long history of community service across the nation."

Currently, the Brookings Chapter is made up of only 34 members. Boekelheide and Karmody believe this is an advantage as it allows members to get to know one another easily.

The group meets every third Wednesday in the Harold's Crest Room of the Student Union. Members cannot be inducted until the first semester of their junior year and are required to maintain a 3.0 grade point average. Seven committees exist to help distrubute responsibilities.

Fundraisers to support the Mortar Board's cause are being held. Members sold leis at the Hobo Day Parade and at SDSU's Cavorts production.

Mortar Board makes the Collegian *with its "Reading is Leading" community service initiative. (*Collegian, *October 27, 1999 story)*

dence and their self-respect. If we learn to really respect ourselves, we will automatically respect others.

I lived in Wecota Hall from the fall of 1932 until the fall of 1943, when all the residence halls were taken over by the Army and Air Force units. During those years of the depression, dust storms and then the war, I had a unique opportunity to observe and share students' lives intimately. State has always seemed to attract the right kind of young people, particularly during those years of stress. They were motivated, worked hard and enthusiastically on student affairs, and had a service motif in their souls. Out of financial need, they all worked at some job and yet were generous with their time in planning worthwhile activities. They took real pride in their themes and decorations for the Hobo Parade, Coed Balls, formal dinners and dances, or teas, participation in "Rabbit Rarities," Girls Band, Chorus and all the organization sponsored activities.

I was overwhelmed at times by students' ingenuity when money was so scarce. I remember well the senior woman who made a lovely evening gown of black satin, trimmed with a single bold appliquéd red velvet poppy, accented with a few sequins on the flower stem and leaves. It covered two-thirds of the length of her gown. It was a masterpiece of simple lines and exquisite design, which could still be appreciated in today's high fashion market. Even a president's wife made a lovely formal out of a white satin, embroidered nightgown.

The rewards of sharing students' lives were endless for me—and occasionally comic. One coed haunted my office on the days of formal dances, because she wanted to give me a manicure, which, incidentally, I could not afford in those lean years. Another coed did all the artwork for yearly brochures, which contained the regulations of the day, because I helped her overcome a drinking problem. Someone told her that a beer shampoo was good for the hair, and subsequently she became overly fond of drinking the stuff. On the morning after Pear Harbor, I was making Christmas cards in the Art Department with a linoleum block cut for me by a student whom I had encouraged to pursue a career in art, despite her very serious health problem of multiple sclerosis. Another coed emptied mousetraps for me because of my phobia. Hundreds of cards have come from her since.

Half a dozen of those young women have become writers with published historical novels, children's books, and professional writers in many fields. I also met first rate artists, fashion designers, an authority on breeding horses and many talented, dedicated teachers, engineers, nurses, architects, pharmacists, horticulturists, and a far larger number of mothers and homemakers, who later sent their teenagers to State. Occasionally their offspring seemed to have more personal problems than their parents because of changing times, peer pressures and more money.

I had the satisfaction of sharing my shelf of poetry books with students who had never felt the thrill of reading good poetry. They learned to love Tagore, Yrbian, Lew Sarrett, Elizabeth B. Browning, and more. Over the years, I recall that at least three coeds who slipped poems under my office door, expressing their appreciation for my assistance with their problems. One was titled "Conch Shell," and in it, the student compared her life to a conch shell, rolled to and fro by the waves, endlessly and with no purpose in life, until I came into her life. It was a beautiful tribute which I shall never forget. Some students could express themselves better through poetry, rather than prose or face to face. Alas, I do not recall any of my protégés being as fascinated as I was with making hats. I could not afford name hats, and so I made my own. Occasionally, a coed would make a hat to accent a dress or suit, but it was routine and not a love affair like mine. The students never ignored my hats and sometimes their comments changed my perception of my design. One said, "Dean, you look

Dean Volstorff with hat at Board of Control meeting. (1941 Jack Rabbit photo)

as though you have either been in a fight or are looking for one." I had thought the asymmetric design quite good until that moment.

Exploring the secrets of a young person's mind is a fascinating experience. There are the bright, creative parts, and the dark, shadowy ones, so very difficult for a stranger to fathom. There is always the danger of discovering too much and creating a dependency or alienation. There is a point beyond which no counselor can go, unless she is certain she is invited and trusted to explore further by the owner of that wonderful machine—the human mind. I have been appalled on occasion by the dark, mysterious depths of human misery and agony, which lay secret in the innermost recesses of the mind. Where suicides are contemplated and sought as an answer to what that young person deemed as a deadened or impossible burden to continuing life. I can truthfully say that I have shared in the agonies and the ecstasies in the lives of many of State's young people—stories of their sweethearts, brothers or fathers safe from war, that first job, scholarships, engagements and sparkling diamonds, and more.

My joy in counseling became diluted in the late sixties and early seventies because of the rise of drug use. I lost my feeling of closeness to the students, because their secrets were now a matter of law enforcement concern. Anyone who has ever worked with a drug-related problem knows the anguish and feeling of frustration at this worst possible abuse of the human body and mind. Fortunately for me, I retired in 1973 before the problem became rampant. But even before then, I saw the way drug abuse removed the privileges of my relationship with students. I was responsible to the authorities, and nothing in my previous experience had prepared me for facing a young woman who had a serious drug problem. I prayerfully hope that drugs are becoming less of a campus problem today, but I am still very concerned about the excessive alcohol consumption and the barhopping culture of today's young people.

Life became far more complicated in South Dakota during the last 20 years I spent at State. I knew all the FBI agents ever stationed in the area, and I discovered an undercover world that I never knew existed. Because I had been at State so long, I was used as a reference frequently by the FBI. Some of my earlier experiences were rather bizarre during World War II, but they were so limited compared to the more recent contacts. One agent burned a couple of marijuana cigarettes in an ashtray in my office to help me to recognize the aroma of marijuana, somewhat to the consternation of my secretary.

What Makes A Young Woman Unforgettable?

I have many memories of my students. Most are personal, far too personal to be shared in a public way. But over the years and after thousands of conversations with female students, I believe I may understand them. At the very least, I know what makes a young woman memorable.

"I did but see her passing by, and yet I love her until I die." No one is sure to whom these haunting lines were addressed, but since the beginning of time, there have been women like that, women who seem to have been born with a grace and charm that makes them live on forever in the hearts of those who know them.

Helen of Troy and Cleopatra, Sarah Bernhardt and Elizabeth Barrett Browning, Stephen Foster's "Jeanie with the light brown hair" and Edgar

Allen Poe's forever mourned young bride, the lost "Lenore," these lovely women and many more inhabit the pages of history, glowing with life.

Cleopatra caused men to throw away kingdoms for her. To prove that nothing is changed, modern times brought us Princess de Rethy, for whom King Leopold renounced the crown of Belgium. This sort of thing happens to ordinary women, too, women who will never see a throne room but who pass like a spring wind through the lives of all of us, leaving behind them a sense that something has happened, that for some mysterious reason life will never be the same again.

Many years ago I read the story of a young man out walking in New York who passed the window of a travel agency. He halted in his tracks, turned and came back. In the window was a poster and on it was a girl. Dark, slim, intense, she was pictured against the background of her homeland. Try as he would, the young man could not forget her. Eventually he came back to the agency full of questions. Discovering that she came from Israel, he dropped his work, took a ship to Israel, found the girl and married her.

What makes a woman unforgettable? Why does one woman have this magic while others, though kind and attractive, pass through the lives of the people they meet and are gone? It takes many characteristics: sex appeal, for example, and beauty, and warmth.

"There are people," said the French essayist, Raoul de Roussey de Sales, "who create about themselves a certain warmth of personality; who transmit to others their particular emotional atmosphere; who show you how to long to suffer, to be happy, to laugh at the humorous things in life."

The unforgettable woman is like that. You know that she is aware of you, not as a fort for her allies but as a person in your own right. Her mind is hospitable to your ideas, her heart open to your joys and sorrows. She is not an onlooker on life. She is in the middle of it. She has a natural love affair with life. She belongs to the moment she is in.

In the court of France three hundred years ago, there was such a woman. Her name was Ninon de Lenclos, notable for her amours and later for social leadership. Some of the greatest men of the century loved her; indeed, she is said to have bewitched three generations of men in a single family, and the most interesting women of France were her devoted friends. The most wonderful thing about her, everyone said, was her eager delight in everything around her. A thousand times a day she would say "I enjoy; I enjoy."

Conversely, the people who fail to lodge in the heart are often those who are afraid of any form of surrender to experience. Many single women don't really want to become involved in any significant relation with a man. Either painfully shy, brittle or aggressive, some women, because of their own painful inability to connect with life, acquire the habit of cynicism and disparagement. Always belittling, they take the edge from every joy, as if constantly biting a sour apple. Presented with a lovely dream, they advise you to come down to earth. Unresponsive women comfort themselves with the thought that the responsive ones merely flatter the ego.

An unforgettable woman brings life; she makes people feel that they are real. Because she is so alive herself, she gives the people she is with a sense of life. Intrigued and curious, such women greet us with honest inquiry, with genuine desire to know what we are like, and it is as though doors spring ajar. The unforgettable woman has a genius for discovering what is worthwhile in another person.

Paradoxically, the unforgettable woman has a deep core of aloneness and privacy and respects these qualities in others. She has a sense of personal security—an inner freedom. She has a satisfying existence in her own mind and imagination that she need not always be entertained. She has self-respect and a quality of serenity. Her mind and her heart are too full to allow room for malicious gossip, for endless debates about clothes and appearance and trivia. Her self-respect is too real to permit indulgence in vanity.

Contrary to folklore, the unforgettable woman is nearly always so to women as well as men. Ninon de Lenclos was sought after in her old days by as many women as by men. Most women of stature have deep, warm friendships with women.

A few years after WW II a friend returned and married the girl he had met only once before he left. "My wife is unforgettable," he said, "she is mysterious. I will never know her. To me that is the most wonderful quality in a woman." A young theologian wrote, "woman is the variable to a man's constant."

In the great love poems the mysterious quality of a woman is celebrated. "We love people in proportion to their degree of strangeness to us," wrote Baudelaire (1821-67 French poet and critic). It is this same quality that attracts people to the Mona Lisa. They stand in front of it, longer than anywhere else, murmuring and admiring, because they don't know what she's thinking and they wish they did.

An unforgettable woman is mysterious but also honest. This is not as difficult as it seems. Mystery and an honest response come alike from the most unforgettable of all qualities, genuineness. The woman who is herself cannot thereby be anyone else. Because no one is like her, she is a mystery to be solved. Because she is not afraid to like what she likes, she is an honest and responsive person to enjoy.

An unforgettable woman is also feminine, an elusive trait. The woman who keeps pushing her femininity isn't really feminine at all. The really feminine woman isn't proving anything. She isn't always getting into the conversation. She doesn't try to make you notice her or her clothes. But when a man is with her, he feels like a man. A very womanly woman has tenderness for a man. She never thinks of herself as engaged in a head to head struggle to get what is coming to her. She likes men, respects and admires what they are trying to achieve, has no resentful bitterness towards them, hopes to make them happy.

She is the kind of person who loves to love others. What makes a woman feminine is tenderness and concern and the willingness to sacrifice for others. What every man in his heart of hearts wants most of all is a woman who will comfort him, to whom he can go when he is tired, to whom he can take his frustrations and his failures, the hopes that are ashes, the lights that have gone out. She will also share his ecstasies.

An unforgettable woman must also be intelligent. Before World War II, says Professor Mirra Kamorovsky of Barnard College in her book "Women in the Modern World," about half of the coeds reported that when they went out with men they felt they often had to underplay their knowledge and intelligence, and also that their families discouraged their being "too intellectual" for fear of hurting their marriage prospects. How many women hid their Phi Beta Kappa key or never admitted to having a scholarship? Today, however, many college women tell me they are concerned about being smart enough to keep up with their preferred boyfriends. The emphasis now is most of all on companionship.

Interestingly enough, the best-loved women of history have almost without exception been able to talk intelligently with the men who sought their company. In the intervals of love-making, women like George Sand (who wrote 60 novels and 25 produced plays) and Mime de Maintenon talked with the men they loved about religion and politics, music and poetry, and were often responsible for great insights on wise and useful decisions. An intelligent woman, like an intelligent man, is a delight to be with.

If a woman's intelligence is the whetstone on which she hones the little barbs which destroy a man, if it drives her away from the people she purportedly loves and persuades her to think of nothing but how to get ahead in the world, she'll be unforgettable all right, but not in a way that can give her much joy. But if, on the other hand, her intelligence is an adjunct to the subtler understanding of the heart, if it helps her to build a bridge between a man's thought and hers; if, when he talks to her, he finds himself thinking more brilliantly and profoundly than before, then he will remember her, and her intelligence, with warmth and delight and go out of his way to see her again. Old Mother Nature intended for a woman to be a complement and a supplement to man, completing and reinforcing each other in a very special way.

Victorian though it may sound, a woman is unforgettable because she is good. Amused male voices might rise in protest as they think of experiences best left unrecorded. But for the most part, the women who have lived in history have been good women, not always conventional perhaps, but honorable, loving, courageous and generous.

Indeed, the woman who lacks these qualities has a short tenure on charm. Luckily for the human race, goodness is more imperishably beautiful than anything else is. Pettiness, selfishness, meanness and greed take very little time to inscribe their unlovely handiwork on a woman's face. "As women grow older there is written on their faces, beyond assistance from all artifice, not only what life has brought to them but what they have brought to life," says John Mason Brown. Many men today wish aloud that the woman they met were "gentlemen." As one college president once said: "Women don't smoke like gentlemen." Civility and service are going out of style.

I suspect the real reason more women are not warm and alive in their responses is that they refuse to take their share of being hurt. They'd rather pussyfoot around the edges of life than leap into it and take what comes. Suspecting people's motives, they'd rather lose the happiness of intimacy than give another human being the gift of trust. The woman who is capable of being greatly loved is the brave one. She leaps into the sea of life, trusting the people she meets, bravely taking what comes her way, and never, in small and frightened pride, counts the respective value of what another human being has done for her and she for him.

Finally, the unforgettable woman makes other people feel larger than life. She has a superlative gift of persuading people that they are more than they thought they were. The more perceptive men are, the more they look first of all for the woman who can so enlarge their lives.

"When you're with a woman you really know and trust," said a thoughtful political science friend who also wrote poetry in his spare time, "you say and do things you've always wanted to but somehow couldn't bring yourself to say and do with your every day friends." In the end, the most unforgettable woman is the one who leads the spirit out of its hiding place.

Interestingly enough, the qualities I have mentioned are also, in large part, the qualities, which make a great person, male or female. They are imperishable. They do not vanish with the years, nor do life's pains and sorrows destroy them.

The sad part of it is that you can't go about trying to be an unforgettable woman. Any woman, who spends all her time wondering whether or not she is unforgettable, whether or not she is lovable, is certainly neither. Nor can many women blaze throughout the pages of their time, bright in the memory of thousands of people. But perhaps it is a greater achievement for a woman to remain, through all the toils and miseries of daily life, unforgettable to one man.

Young couples now can expect to spend more than four decades of life together before one or the other dies. That is a long time to stay in a man's heart, his love, and his memory. And it must be sorrowfully pointed out that not many women achieve it.

Yet every woman could be unforgettable to the man who loved and chose her. In the end, the woman a man remembers is the woman he needs, the one who comforts, the one who can give him security and fruitful experience. And the more a woman seeks to live naturally by the best of herself, the more she loves, the more gentle she is in her judgments, the richer her married life, the warmer her responsiveness, the more she will be the woman needed, and therefore, the woman unforgettable.

And last, but most important, let her have a positive philosophy of life.

Let our unforgettable woman be a positive person who emphasizes the good in our very imperfect world! Be glad to be a woman. Being a female one cannot change, but being a lady is an achievement. A lady is a woman who makes it easy for a man to be a gentleman. We must adjust to changing times and still hold to unchanging principles that result in our personal moral standards.

That lesson, if no other, is the one I hope my students keep close to their hearts.

UNFORGETTABLE YOUNG WOMEN REMEMBER DEAN VOLSTORFF

Five representative and unforgettable young women share their memories of Dean Volstorff in the Epilogue.

Eleanore Christopherson Cranston Roscoe
Home Economics, Brookings, S.D.; Home Economics Club and Rifle Team. (1933 Jack Rabbit photo)

Susan Smith Schutz
Pharmacy, Kimball, S.D.; Pharmaceutical Society secretary, Women's Self Governing Association, Newman Club president, Stakota Club, Rooter Club queen, Varsity sweetheart, Union Board, Prexy Club, Guidon, Senior Prom queen. (1946 Jack Rabbit photo)

Patricia Clancy Leiferman
Home Economics, Madison, S.D.; Little International, Stakota Club, Home Economic Club, Guidon, Phi Upsilon Omicron and Newman Club. (1954 Jack Rabbit photo)

Barbara K. Strandell
Arts and Science, Watertown, S.D.; Forensics, Dorm Officer, Students' Association president, Who's Who and Lutheran Students Association. (1972 Jack Rabbit photo)

Susan Stockland Olson
Arts and Science, Wakonda, S.D.; Associated Women Students president, College Republicans, Spanish Club, Dance Club, Resident Assistant and Who's Who. (1973 Jack Rabbit photo)

UNFORGETTABLE YOUNG MEN REMEMBER DEAN VOLSTORFF

Two representative and unforgettable young men share their memories of Dean Volstorff in the Epilogue.

Robert F. Karolevitz
General Science, Bremerton, Wash.;
Printonian Club, Newman Club, Blue Key.
(1948 Jack Rabbit photo)

Arvid O. Peterson
Engineering, Watertown, S.D.:
Statesmen, Hobo Day Committee,
Students' Association president and
AFROTC.
(1964 Jack Rabbit photo)

DEAN VOLSTORFF WAS CHARM AND GRACE

In the fall of 1932, I was thrilled at my becoming a freshman in Home Economics at South Dakota State. My sister, Irene Christopherson Jacobsen, had preceded me from 1922-1926. Dean Edith Pierson resided at the "Practice Cottage" where seniors had a live-in period to gain experience in child-care, housekeeping, menu planning, and preparation.

To me the campus was so beautiful and inspiring. I lived at 1029 Seventh Avenue North and remembered the building of the Campanile with its beautiful chimes and revolving light. All of my childhood I had walked up to watch "Christy's" marvelous marching band and listened to the music of his superb organization. No one to compare with him unless it was Sousa himself!

That year of 1932, the college had the great good fortune to acquire, as Dean of Women, Vivian Volstorff. Many of my Home Economics friends lived in the dorms, Wecota and Wenona, where Dean Volstorff and Mrs. Knight also resided. The Home Economics girls were given the opportunity of providing the petite sandwiches and cakes for "Teas" that Dean Volstorff organized from time to time. We all had our turn of "pouring" from the lovely silver pots at each end of a table covered in fine linens with beautiful flowers and appointments, a wonderful means of teaching good manners and hostess skills.

Retired homemaker who resides in Bakersfield, Calif. (Eleanore Christopherson Cranston Roscoe photo)

My first and continued impression of Dean Volstorff was of her charm and grace in her movements and contacts with all students. Her flair and style of dress were impeccable. The gowns she wore for dancing were absolutely gorgeous, and her street clothes and hats so unique and becoming. I was sure that her clothing had not been purchased in Brookings, and in recent years when I have had the pleasure of visiting her at Brookview Manor, she admitted to having been a long time customer of Neiman Marcus! I told her that I hoped she had saved her gowns for a museum exhibit somewhere on the Campus.

It is my own impression that she instigated our Maypole Winding, Rabbit Rarities, campus dances in the Armory on weekends, and many social events that are sorely lacking for present students. No more proms, balls or school weekend dances? What a shame that this wonderful school spirit and activity has been lost.

The wonderful Marghab Linen Collection and Harvey Dunn Gallery are real treasures without duplication anywhere. We who know South Dakota State University have much to be proud of and it's a grand place to return to visit and admire. Such happy memories. I love my "State" magazine and read it cover to cover.

—Eleanore Christopherson Cranston
Roscoe Ex '33

I Will Always Be Grateful.

V3, as we secretly called her, was my only hope of acquiring some sort of refinement or sophistication when I arrived at SDSU in 1942. As a pharmacy student, I missed the teas and dinners that the Home Economics students had but Dean Volstorff's full, soft voice reminded me my midwest twang could use some modeling. I was a member of the Available Eight who lived with the Dean in a house during the war. I recall one evening I was pounding out "Old Man More" on the piano and the girls were singing on high volume when a knock on the door was finally heard. It was the Dean asking for quietness as she entertained the President of the College at dinner. She constantly reminded us of what was "appropriate" and what was "inappropriate." For such a gracious model, I will always be grateful.

—*Susan King Schutz '46*

Retired stock broker who resides in Aberdeen, S.D. (Susan Smith Schutz photo)

"UNFORGETTABLE!"

Writer who lives in Mission Hill, S.D. (Robert F. Karolevitz photo)

As a returning veteran after World War II, I took essay tests from Dean Volstorff in her "Contemporary Europe" class. As I recall, I wrote voluminous "answers," even if I didn't know what I was talking about. Vivian knew I was giving her a "snow job," but I think she gave me an A anyway, mostly because of my creativity and just plain devilishness.

We had that kind of relationship. She was an outstanding teacher, and I respected how she handled us older guys who had to come back after the war to finish up. Even though she was my senior by more than 20 years, we always met, not as the Dean and student, but as adults.

What I liked most about her, though, was that she was teasable. For instance, we kidded her about the hats she made and wore. I remember that when I wrote the copy for the 1947 *Jack Rabbit*—and the Students' Association annual dinner, in particular—I said something like "Miss Volstorff wore one of her famous hat creations and was jabbed in the coiffure twice by a fellow who mistook her bonnet for his vegetable salad." It was what I could write about Dean Volstorff and get away with.

However, before the war—in the early forties—we treated 3V with a different but special respect; because, after all, she was not only the Dean of Women, but she dangled the keys at Wecota Hall to signal the last minute before the doors were closed for the night. Both the guys and the gals remember her especially for that.

While I was a student for just a tenth of her four decades on the campus, my memories of Vivian include her lectures on etiquette to incoming freshmen; judging Hobo Day beards;

dancing with Duane McDowell, my roommate who was one of her many student dates; her educational devotion to the *New York Times*; and, of course, how she worried about all of us, maybe more than our parents did.

I'm sure she wasn't thinking of herself when she wrote about the "unforgettable woman" in the last chapter of this book, but for those of us who have known her, she was describing herself.

She truly is "unforgettable!"

—*Bob Karolevitz '47*

DROP A PEBBLE IN THE WATER

Dean Volstorff had such a positive impact on the lives of so many students, men as well as women, who attended State College during the decades she served as Dean of Women.

I feel the following poem, "Drop a Pebble in the Water" by James W. Foley, is a very fitting tribute to this kind, gracious, caring *grand dame* of SDSU, who was a friend to everyone with whom she had contact.

Entrepreneur/Homemaker who resides in Bridgewater, S.D. (Patricia Clancy Leiferman photo)

Drop a Pebble in the Water

Drop a pebble in the water;
just a splash, and it is gone;
But there's half-a-hundred ripples
circling on and on and on,
Spreading, spreading from the center,
flowing on out to the sea.
And there is no way of telling
where the end is going to be.

Drop a word of cheer and kindness;
just a flash and it is gone;
But there's half-a-hundred ripples
circling on and on and on,
Bearing hope and joy and comfort
on each splashing, dashing wave
Till you wouldn't believe the volume
of the one kind word you gave.

Drop a word of cheer and kindness;
in a minute you forget;
But there's gladness still a-swelling,
and there's joy a circling yet,
And you've rolled a wave of comfort
whose sweet music can be heard
Over miles and miles
just by dropping one kind word.

—Submitted, with many fond memories,
Patricia (Clancy) Leiferman '54

My Two "Moms"

My first memory of Miss Volstorff was at Orientation Days in the fall of 1959. She spoke to the college freshmen and told all of us what was expected of us young men while at college and the rules involving visitation of "her" young women. Twice a year there would be an open house at the dorms and all doors would be left open during the visitation. She informed us of the weekday and weekend hours of the women's dorms and that they would be strictly enforced. However, she did so with humorous examples of times when she had to get involved with young men who seemed to want their own set of rules. Right away I liked her and respected her and knew that she was going to be our Mother away from home.

During my sophomore year I was elected to the Board of Control as the engineering representative. Prof. Orlin Walder, Dean of Men, and Miss Volstorff, Dean of Women, were the advisors. We met every Monday evening. I was absolutely amazed at the way these two worked together to give guidance to each of us in all the many situations that needed our attention. Especially of interest was their knowledge of Hobo Day and all the activities that lead up to that Greatest Single-Day Event in South Dakota. From their experience they would predict what to expect in behavior of the students, especially the night before Hobo Day. We were all assigned locations to "mingle with the students downtown and on campus to help direct the activities of students to a positive conclusion." And it worked!

My junior year I was elected President of the Students' Association and presided over the Board of Control. I would never have been

District Manager, Farmer's Insurance Group who resides in Coon Rapids, Minn. (Arvid O. Peterson photo)

able to complete that task without Prof. and V.V.'s guidance. They were my Dad and Mom away from home and I relied on their knowledge on many occasions. I don't ever remember any conflicts in our relationships primarily because they were so good at explaining and discussing any differences in opinion in such an understanding way.

Following college I would visit the campus many times since my brother Harold lived in Aurora. On one occasion I brought my year-and-one-half-old son, Scott, with me. Miss Volstorff held him and placed him on her desktop. She said, "Now what can the Dean of Women possibly find to entertain this young boy?" Just then Scott reached for her scotch tape dispenser. She gave him the roll of tape and he proceeded to handcuff himself with all that tape. She then lovingly and carefully cut him free. Scott attended SDSU and wanted to visit Miss Volstorff and tease her about the tape experience but she had retired. However, recently he visited her and related the incident to her and she said she remembered it well and that she was pleased to see he was such a fine looking young man.

In the late sixties, I visited Miss Volstorff after returning from Vietnam. She was so concerned about all of "her boys" having to serve in another war. Her compassion and understanding of the horrors of war were so real. Again I was impressed with her knowledge and how well she could remember so many people and their experiences.

In the early 1980s the Statesmen, men's singing group, had a reunion with an afternoon practice and concert. The "old" guys would be singing with the present student men's group. I called Miss Volstorff to make sure she would be attending. She said she hadn't been getting around as much lately and would not be able to attend especially since the concert was upstairs in the old library and she couldn't climb those long steps anymore. I told her that there would be many of her "boys" returning and very disappointed if she wasn't there and we would personally carry her up those stairs if necessary. She agreed to come and we went to get her. We used an employee elevator to skip the stairs. I told former and guest director Dr. John Rezatto about our special guest and when he introduced her she received a standing ovation. We also dedicated a song to her. It was great to see the smile on her face when all of "her young men" were serenading her.

Recently my mother became a resident at Brookview Manor. When looking over a directory of residents I was thrilled to see the name of Vivian V. Volstorff. I immediately went to her room and introduced my mother and myself. I said, "Miss Volstorff, I am Arvid Peterson and I would like to introduce you to my mother, Agnes Peterson, who is also a resident here. I graduated from State in 1963 and was Students' Association President. You may not remember me because it's been a few years since I last saw you". She said, "Oh yes, I remember you, Arvid, and I am pleased to meet you, Mrs. Peterson." Mom asked her to call her Agnes and Miss Volstorff said please call me Vivian. She than said I could tell you a lot about your son but some of it will remain untold. Mom said the same was true. It was good to have my two "Moms" together. They are great women who have influenced my life and I am so thankful for their support and the wonderful memories.

—Arvid O. Peterson '63

VV At The Crossroads

Consultant/Trainer who resides in St. Paul, Minn. (Barbara Strandell photo)

My first memory of Dean Volstorff begins in the Fall of 1969. I heard that the Dean of Women was having a "cozy" or tea for freshman women. This was, apparently, a tradition at SDSU. The purpose was twofold: introduce herself to us and, explain the ways in which she could be of assistance to coeds during our college years. Not a bad idea, I thought. But, I had also heard that one was expected to wear white gloves and a dress to the event. Well, that ended any interest I had in attending the cozy. I certainly did not come to college to wear gloves and dress—I had had enough of that at home!

So, I didn't actually meet the mythical Dean Volstorff until I was elected to the Board of Control (BOC) my sophomore year.

There she was—at "the table" along with the Dean of Men, Prof. Walder. As the faculty advisors to the BOC they attended every meeting. I must admit, I was impressed and a bit intimidated by Dr. Volstorff's grandeur. An imposing figure with large earrings, lipstick (who ever wore *that* to BOC meetings?), her partially grayed hair pulled back—Golda Maier style (I thought at the time), a knit dress with brass buttons, a twinkle in her eyes and those trademark dimples that made the entire room light up when she smiled. And no white gloves. I was relieved.

VV—what Paul Franich, the editor of the *Collegian*, and I affectionately called her, seemed surprisingly open to new proposals by some of us who were considered more "radical." She did, however, always advise caution. Oftentimes VV would float our ideas to key administrators, thus laying the groundwork for a proposal to sail through a faculty committee or secure Dr. Briggs' approval. Since she had a terrific relationship with the President, we trusted her feedback and insight. It certainly wasn't always a love feast; there were many times when she did not agree with our proposals.

In the early '70s some of the biggest topics of discussion in student government were: more coed dormitories, eliminating curfews, beer on campus, common course curriculum, not sending grades to parents, voter registration, funding for a new library, and, of course, the war in Vietnam. The role of a traditional "Dean of Women" was in conflict with the very idea we were most passionate about: eliminating the University's role of *"en loco parentis."* We felt that if we were adult enough to fight in a war and vote, we did not need substitute parents on campus.

I watched Dean Volstorff make this difficult transition. She became more of an advisor/advocate than "mother figure."

I was elected Students' Association (SA) President my junior year. Not since World War II had a female been honored in such a way. I was able to beat out two formidable male opponents and receive more votes than their combined vote totals. Dr. Volstorff invited me to her office shortly after the election. She expressed absolute elation over my victory and told me that she had secretly wanted me to win but had to remain neutral during the campaign. She told me that although we differed in our approaches to things—me being more direct and impatient, she being more diplomatic and patient, that she was confident that we could work together. She said that, more than anything, she wanted me to be successful;

it was a turbulent time and a woman might have a greater challenge.

From that point on, our relationship blossomed. She advised and mentored and eventually we became trusted friends. Vivian Volstorff taught me how to be more discreet in my dealing with the administration; how to lead with my wit, friendly personality (rather than my confrontational one) and intellect in persuading faculty to the students' point of view. She made suggestions on how to "work the back of the room" as well as the front. Though I was an independent person, I liked the personal attention she paid to me; was I getting enough sleep, was I skipping too many classes, was I working too hard, maybe I shouldn't smoke?

At my BOC meetings, she and I developed a non-verbal method of communicating. When Dean Volstorff saw or heard something that I didn't notice she would tip me off by nodding until I recognized her. Then, she would say "Madam Chairman, I think we need to talk about this some more." When I needed her to proffer a different view or affirm a past decision, I would make a statement and bend my head toward her and she would take the baton. She helped me understand the importance of preparing an organized agenda, being more familiar with the material and issues than anyone else, remaining objective as long as I had the gavel in hand and mastering Robert's Rules of Order to maximize efficiency and fairness throughout the BOC meetings.

In the midst of our differences, we always managed to respect each other's positions. One of the topics about which we had a major conflict was teacher evaluation. Students posited the view that if we were paying for an education and the teacher was lousy, we should either get our money back or the teacher should be held accountable. We also believed that students should have significant input regarding the tenure decision. Dean Volstorff, embracing the erudite tradition of higher education, simply could not see students having much to say about faculty performance. The students gained a little ground by getting a non- voting student on each review committee and by periodically conducting teacher evaluations. VV's side didn't lose too much; the system of tenure remains much the same at SDSU and schools across the country. She wasn't alone!

When the BOC elected to choose our own advisers rather than have them assigned by administration, I knew I was going to miss VV. Though I was a supporter of that change, I was truly saddened by her departure. She accepted the decision and left in her normal style with grace and great aplomb.

During my tenure as SA President, SDSU received approval to build a new Student Union. We elected student representatives who were very much involved in the design of the building. VV helped. I remember our selecting the purple, orange, red, blue and gold color schemes and themes for the walls, carpeting and furniture. But the thing that I am most proud of regarding the new student union was the decision we (the Student Union Board of Directors) made to name the ballroom in honor of Dean Volstorff. Her great legacy will always be remembered by that naming. The Volstorff Ballroom is a fitting tribute to a grand lady who always loved to dance and loved to be engaged with student life whether it was in her History classroom, student government activities, mortar board club, or the sororities. She had a definite influence on my formative years. And I am a better person and a better leader for having known her.

After I graduated and she retired, I made several visits to her home. She welcomed me, took an interest in my career and was comfortable giving me personal advice: "Don't you think you would feel better if you quit chewing your fingernails?"—yes, and I did!

My only regret is that I didn't know that she had an extensive poetry library. I was then and am now an avid reader and writer of poetry. Perhaps our next visit will be filled with a different kind of poetry than the kind we shared in those turbulent times of the late '60s and early '70s.

—Barbara K. Strandell '73

From Meat And Potatoes To Petit Four

On the wall of my living room there is a collection of cobalt blue Danish plates and to this day, I get a smile on my face and in my heart as I note the one with the 1972 date. Even though it matches the other plates in my collection, I consider it a bit misplaced. Instead of being in my home, perhaps it would be better placed in my office and hanging on the wall beside my degrees from South Dakota State University. That plate was a gift to me from Miss. Volstorff after having been under her advisement for two years as an officer for the Association of Women Students. When she gave me that Christmas gift during my second year of working with her, I felt very honored and a little like "I might be passing" Miss Volstorff's approval and her informal course on how to be a young lady, leader, and scholar. Although I never formally was in one of her classes, she took the time to call me to her office, monitor my personal and academic well being, and offer me bits of advice, direction, and kindness. I would leave her office knowing that I was not simply an ID number and that my thoughts and actions made a difference. She would take time to groom me for my AWS offices and for life. She would call me to her office, visit with me for awhile, assess my well being and knowledge, do her best to teach me some points of etiquette and fundamental "must knows" of life, and then send me on my way.

Soon after having been elected to an office in an organization that was under her advisement, the phone rang in my Binnewies Hall dorm room. I was not in the room at the time and a girl passing my open door answered the

Middle School Counselor who resides in Colton, S.D. (Susan Stockland Olson photo)

call. The word spread fast "Find Sue Stockland! Miss Volstorff, the Dean of Women, is on the phone and wants to talk to her." Was I in trouble? Was I somebody a little bit important? Who knows? The fact was that Miss Volstorff wanted me to come to her office the following afternoon to meet with her. I was nervous! It would have been 24 hours of less stress if I could have reported immediately to her office after the phone call.

I arrived a few minutes early for our meeting and did need to wait as she finished meeting with another person. My stomach was in knots and the 5-10 minute wait seemed to be more like an hour of waiting. As she said farewell to the student leaving her office and she welcomed me, my borderline panic attack subsided and a new adventure and friendship in life was about to begin.

I can not help but wonder what thoughts went through her mind that day. She was well-educated, confident and a worldly woman from Chicago. The piece of clay that entered her office was far from that semblance. I was a naïve 18-year-old who had barely been beyond the borders of South Dakota, was a middle child in a family of 10, and had spent my life living in the same house on the same farm where my dad raised pigs.

I had attended country school for eight years before high school in Wakonda where I joined a class of 27 students. My only claims to fame were that I had received numerous awards in 4-H and was the 1970 South Dakota Pork Queen. Thanks to a city dwelling English grandmother who relentlessly sought to instill good manners in her grandchildren and thanks to my parents and to Doyce Freiberg, the South Dakota Pork Council Secretary, and

LaVerne (Korty) Kortan, the SDSU Swine Specialist, who took me to numerous small South Dakota farming towns for Jubilee and Centennial parades and celebrations, I did get some lessons in etiquette and on being gracious. But, it was not until Miss Volstorff entered my life that I was exposed to petit four and some higher level specifics on being a gracious hostess. It was from her that I learned the art of hats, gloves, and finesse. Miss Volstorff walked me through hosting a faculty tea and spring formal and she taught me the things that I would need to teach my date about being a gentleman and starting the first dance at the spring formal.

As a shy pharmacy student, my date almost backed out when he learned that starting the first dance would be his responsibility. Additionally, he was expected to invite Miss Volstorff to the floor for a dance. He pondered for two weeks prior to the dance what dance floor topics they could discuss. Besides, in his mind he did not know how to dance well enough to dance with the Dean of Women. Like me, he was nervous until he met her and then all was well.

Miss Volstorff modeled for many of us in ways that only she could do. She reached out and took in others, and me. As South Dakota students, she opened our eyes. She sought to give us awareness, to broaden our horizons and visions. She taught skills and social graces.

She was never one of my professors but she was always my teacher. Thank you Dean Volstorff, for taking the time and for making a difference in my life.

—Sue Stockland Olson '74 & '78

Order Form
for *Winds of Change*

*Name*____

Address ____

City _______________________ *State* ______ *Zip* ________

Telephone ____

Number of books ____ *@ $15.00 plus S&H of $2.95 =* ________

Payment Methods:

___*Check Payable to the SDSU Alumni Association*

___*Please Charge it to my:* ___ *Mastercard* ___ *Visa*

Card # _____________________ *Expiration Date* _________

Signature ____

Send orders to:
Tompkins Alumni Center
PO Box 515
Brookings, SD 57007

For questions, contact:
SDSU Alumni Association
(605) 697-5198 or toll free (888) 735-2257